German Railroads, Jewish Souls

GERMAN RAILROADS, JEWISH SOULS

The Reichsbahn, Bureaucracy, and the Final Solution

CHRISTOPHER R. BROWNING, PETER HAYES,
AND RAUL HILBERG

Published in association with
the United States Holocaust Memorial Museum

berghahn
NEW YORK · OXFORD
www.berghahnbooks.com

First published in 2020 by
Berghahn Books
www.berghahnbooks.com

Certain assertions, arguments, and conclusions contained herein are those of the contributors and do not necessarily reflect the opinions of the United States Holocaust Memorial Museum. This publication appears with the support of the Jack, Joseph and Morton Mandel Center for Advanced Holocaust Studies, United States Holocaust Memorial Museum.

Raul Hilberg's article "German Railroads/Jewish Souls" appeared in the journal *Society*, November 1976, volume 14, issue 1, pp. 60–74, © Springer Science and Business Media, New York, and is reprinted with permission of Springer.

Raul Hilberg's article "The Bureaucracy of Annihilation" from *Unanswered Questions*, edited by François Furet, translated by Benjamin Ivry, translation copyright © 1989 Penguin Random House LLC, is used by permission of Schocken Books, an imprint of the Knopf Doubleday Publishing Group, a division of Penguin Random House LLC. All rights reserved. The same material is used with the additional permission of Éditions du Seuil, publisher of the French edition of the anthology *L'Allemagne nazis et le génocide juif. Colloque de l'Ecole des Hautes Etudes en Sciences Sociales*, © Éditions du Seuil, 1985.

Photos 2 and 5–11 appear with the permission of the United States Holocaust Memorial Museum.
Photo 1 appears with the permission of Bundesarchiv—Federal Archives.
Photo 3 appears with the permission of Sueddeutsche Zeitung Photo.
Photo 4 appears courtesy of Yad Vashem.

Document F.1, "Zwischen Tag und Dunkel," © 1984 Hilde Sherman, published in translation by permission of Liepman, AG, Zurich.
Document F.2, "From Lviv to Bełżec," excerpts in English published with permission of the Judaica Foundation—Center for Jewish Culture, Kraków.

Library of Congress Cataloging-in-Publication Data

Names: Browning, Christopher R., author. | Hayes, Peter, author. | Hilberg, Raul, 1926-2007, author.
Title: German railroads, Jewish souls : the Reichsbahn, bureaucracy, and the Final solution / by Christopher R. Browning, Peter Hayes, and Raul Hilberg.
Description: New York ; Oxford : Berghahn Books, [2019] | Published in association with the United States Holocaust Memorial Museum. | Includes bibliographical references and index.
Identifiers: LCCN 2019014415 (print) | LCCN 2019016158 (ebook) | ISBN 9781789202779 (ebook) | ISBN 9781789202755 (hardback : alk. paper) | ISBN 9781789202762 (pbk. : alk. paper)
Subjects: LCSH: Deutsche Reichsbahn (Germany) | Railroad companies—Germany—History—20th century. | World War, 1939–1945—Deportations. | Holocaust, Jewish (1939–1945) | Railroads and states—Germany—History—20th century.
Classification: LCC HE3080.D4 (ebook) | LCC HE3080.D4 H55 2019 (print) | DDC 940.53/1813—dc23
LC record available at https://lccn.loc.gov/2019014415

British Library Cataloguing in Publication Data

A catalogue record for this book is available from the British Library.

ISBN 978-1-78920-275-5 hardback
ISBN 978-1-78920-276-2 paperback
ISBN 978-1-78920-277-9 ebook

CONTENTS

Photographs follow page 139.

ILLUSTRATIONS

Figures

Tables

Photos

PREFACE

Raul Hilberg was the "founding father" of the academic study of the Holocaust in the United States, and he had profound impact on how this topic has been researched and written about throughout the world. Born in Vienna in 1926, he and his family escaped Europe in the spring of 1939 and, after a brief stay in Cuba, reached the United States on 1 September, the very day Hitler invaded Poland and started World War II.

Hilberg joined the US Army at the age of eighteen and served in Europe before returning home to complete his undergraduate studies at Brooklyn College and his Ph.D. at Columbia. In the course of his education, he encountered three influential scholars who left their imprint: Hans Rosenberg, the expert on Prussian bureaucracy; Salo Baron, the doyen of Jewish history; and Franz Neumann, the author of *Behemoth*, a work that focused not on the personality and ideology of Hitler but on the structure and polycratic nature of the Nazi regime.

In 1956, Hilberg obtained a position in the department of Political Science at the University of Vermont, where he taught courses primarily in the area of international relations and American foreign policy. After numerous rejections, his first book *The Destruction of the European Jews* was published in 1961, the same year the Eichmann trial took place in Jerusalem. Hilberg's major contribution was to portray the Nazi destruction of the European Jews not as a giant pogrom, an orgy of sadism, nor as a descent from civilization into barbarism, but rather as a bureaucratic and administrative process, requiring specialists of all kinds and successfully eliciting participation from virtually every branch of organized German society. Hilberg created an overarching structure for his study through the interplay of two key concepts: a "machinery of destruction" and a "process of destruction." The machinery comprised the four hierarchical power centers Neumann had identified—the party, civil service, military, and industry. The process consisted of three crucial stages—definition, concentration, and annihilation—with each stage accompanied by commensurate expropriation. In *The Destruction of the European Jews*, Hilberg analyzed how the four hierarchies of the "machinery" carried out the successive stages in the "process" throughout the German empire.

Hilberg's self-imposed task was to "grasp how this deed was done." In that pursuit, he turned to a study of what he considered a paradigmatic perpetrator organization—the German railway system or Reichsbahn. Seemingly the most nonpolitical and nonideological of institutions in Nazi Germany, it nonetheless shipped more than half of the victims of the Holocaust to the death camps; quite simply its trains were indispensable to the Final Solution. Working with the most fragmentary documentation, Hilberg revealed how a staff of technocrats facing extreme wartime demands adapted its standard routines to arrange hundreds of one-way charter trains to the death camps, charged per track kilometer at a group rate discount, with children under ten half-price and infants under four generously sent to their deaths cost-free. The German railway men, Hilberg concluded, shipped Jews like cattle but booked them like any other passengers!

Hilberg then directed his attention to an entirely different topic and was singularly responsible for the 1979 publication of the superbly edited English version of *The Warsaw Diary of Adam Czerniakow*. Much already was known about the most notorious and least attractive ghetto leaders, such as the self-important and power-hungry Chaim Rumkowski of Łódź. Through the diary of the head of the Jewish council in Warsaw, English readers now could encounter an entirely different sort of man—a truly tragic figure who rolled his rock of Sisyphus up the hill every day, knowing full well that it would come rolling back down each night. Consumed by a sense of obligation and untouched by megalomania, Czerniakow persevered in his impossible situation until he reached a line he would not cross. When presented with the demand to deport Jewish children, he took poison.

Having devoted much of his scholarly life to analyzing the impersonal structures and processes of the Nazi assault on the European Jews, Hilberg next took another different approach. His book *Perpetrators Victims Bystanders* not only laid out a tripartite scheme and vocabulary of categorization that has left an indelible imprint on the field, but also examined in twenty-four distinct essays, the experience, perspective, and behavior of various subgroups of people within those broad categories, thus proving himself the master of the telling vignette as well as of overarching analytical concepts.

Though he retired from the University of Vermont in 1991, Hilberg was by no means done writing, leaving us with two more very different books: his academic memoirs, *The Politics of Memory: The Journey of a Holocaust*

Historian, and a methodological study, *Sources of Holocaust Research: An Analysis*. Throughout his career he also continued to update *The Destruction of the European Jews*, which appeared in two revised and expanded editions in the United States (1985 and 2003) as well as in numerous foreign translations. He died in 2007 at the age of eighty-one.

Among all of Hilberg's publications, his scholarship on the German Reichsbahn and the Holocaust has been the least accessible to readers of English. For this reason, the other authors of this volume decided to produce a book based upon his two most important articles on this topic. We believe that these articles exemplify in concise form Hilberg's approach to the history and analysis of the Holocaust as well as the craft with which he presented his findings. We hope that by combining a selection of documents and our own historiographical commentaries with these articles—each lightly edited for accuracy and for consistency of spelling, punctuation, capitalization, and use of italics with our contributions—we have provided a book that proves both useful for students, teachers, and researchers and a fitting tribute to a remarkable scholar.

Christopher R. Browning
Peter Hayes

THE BUREAUCRACY OF ANNIHILATION

Raul Hilberg

We are, all of us who have thought and written about the Holocaust, accustomed to thinking of this event as unique. There is no concept in all history like the Final Solution. There is no precedent for the almost endless march of millions of men, women, and children into gas chambers. The systematization of this destruction process sets it aside from all else that has ever happened. Yet if we examine this event in detail, observing the progression of small steps day by day, we see much in the destruction of Jewry that is familiar and even commonplace in the context of contemporary institutions and practices. Basically, the Jews were destroyed as a consequence of a multitude of acts performed by a phalanx of functionaries in public offices and private enterprises, and many of these measures, taken one by one, turn out to be bureaucratic, embedded in habit, routine, and tradition. It is almost a case of regarding the whole upheaval in all of its massiveness as something incredible, and then observing the small components and seeing in them very little that one could not expect in a modern society. One can go further and assert that it is the very mundaneness and ordinariness of these everyday official actions that made the destruction process so crass. Never before had the total experience of a modern bureaucracy been applied to such an undertaking. Never before had it produced such a result.

The uprooting and annihilation of European Jewry was a multi-pronged operation of a highly decentralized apparatus. This was no perpetration by a single department staffed with specialists in destruction. Germany never had a commissariat of Jewish affairs. The machinery of destruction was the organized German society, its ministries, armed forces, party formations, and industry.[1] In democratic countries, we are accustomed to thinking of legislatures as devices that control administrative units, infuse them with power and money, authorize them to undertake action, and by implication, of course, apportion jurisdiction between them. In Nazi Germany, there was no legislature that, like the United States Congress, can create an agency and abolish it. In Nazi Germany, every organization moved on a track of self-assertion. To some of us this may seem like anarchy. How much more remarkable then that this congeries of bureaucratic agencies, these people drawn from every area of expertise, operating without a basic plan, uncoordinated in any central office, nevertheless displayed order, balance, and economy throughout the destruction process.

The apparatus was able to advance unerringly, because there was an inner logic to its measures. A decree defining the term "Jew," expropriations of Jewish property, the physical separation and isolation of the victims, forced labor, deportations, gassings—these were not random moves. The sequence of steps was built in; each was a stage in the development. By 1941, the participating decision-makers themselves became aware that they had been traveling on a determined path. As their assault took on gestalt, its latent structure became manifest. Now they had an overview that allowed them to see a beginning and an end and that prompted them to demand of indigenous administrations in occupied and satellite countries that the "Nuremberg principle" be adopted in the definition of the Jews and that other precedents laid down in Germany be followed in the appropriate order for the accomplishment of a "final solution."[2]

Nothing, however, was simple. Neither the preliminary nor the concluding phases of the destruction process could be traversed without difficulties and complications. The Jewish communities had all been emancipated and they were tied to the Gentile population in countless relationships, from business contacts, partnerships, leases, and employment contracts, to personal friendships and intermarriages. To sever these connections one by one, a variety of measures were necessary, and these actions were taken by specialists who were accountants, lawyers, engineers, or physicians. The questions with which these men were concerned were almost always technical. How was a "Jewish enterprise" to be defined? Where were the borders of a ghetto to be drawn? What was to be the disposition of pension claims belonging to deported Jews? How should bodies be disposed of? These were the problems pondered by the bureaucrats in their memoranda, correspondence, meetings, and discussions. That was the essence of their work.

No organized element of German society was entirely uninvolved in the process of destruction. Yet this very fact, which is virtually an axiom, has been extraordinarily hard to assimilate in descriptions and assessments of the Nazi regime. It is much easier to visualize the role of a propagandist or some practitioner of violence than to appreciate the contribution of a bookkeeper. For this reason, the principal spotlight in postwar years has been placed on the SS and the Gestapo. There is some awareness also of the military, particularly where, as in occupied France, it had made itself conspicuous. Similarly unavoidable was the discovery that an enterprise like I. G. Farben had established branches in Auschwitz. Much less well known, however, are the activities of such faceless components of the destructive machine as the Finance Ministry, which engaged in confiscations, or the armed forces network of armament inspectorates, which was concerned with forced labor, or German municipal authorities that directed or participated in the creation and maintenance of ghettos in Eastern Europe. Two large bureaucracies have remained all but obscure, even though they operated at the very scene of death: the German railroads and the Order Police. This omission should give us pause.

Trains and street police have been common sights in Europe for more than a century. Of all the agencies of government, these two organizations have always been highly visible to every inhabitant of the continent, yet they have been overlooked in the analysis of the Nazi regime. It is as if their very size and ubiquity deflected attention from the lethal operations in which they were so massively engaged. What was the function of the German railroads in the annihilation of the Jews? What tasks did the Order Police perform?

Case I: The Indispensability of the Railroads

In the chain of steps that led to the extinction of millions of Jewish victims, the Reichsbahn, as the German railways were known, carried the Jews from many countries and regions of Europe to the death camps, which were situated on occupied Polish soil. The Jews were passed from one jurisdiction to another: from the civil or military authorities that had uprooted and concentrated them, to the Security Police, which was in charge of rounding them up, to the Reichsbahn, which transported them to the camps where they were gassed. Reichsbahn operations were a crucial link in this process and their significance is underscored by their magnitude. Camps account for most of the Jewish dead, and almost all of the people deported there were moved by rail. The movement encompassed 3 million Jews.

Of course, these transports were but a small portion of the Reichsbahn's business. At its peak, the railway network stretched from Bordeaux to Dnepropetrovsk and points east, and its personnel consisted of a half million civil servants and almost twice as many other employees.[3] In the Reich itself (including Austria, Polish incorporated territory, and the Białystok district), some 130,000 freight cars were being assembled for loading every day.[4] Germany depended on its railroads to carry soldiers and civilians, military cargo, and industrial products throughout the war. A complex functional and territorial division of labor was required to administer these transport programs.

The transport minister, Julius Dorpmüller, held the office from 1937 to the end of the war. The Staatssekretär (state secretary) responsible for railways in the ministry was at first Wilhelm Kleinmann and, from the spring of 1942, Dr. Albert Ganzenmüller, a young, capable engineer and consummate technocrat who was to transport what Albert Speer was to production.[5] Ganzenmüller's central divisions, labeled E (for *Eisenbahn* or railway) included E 1 (Traffic and Tariffs), E 2 (Operations), and L *(Landesverteidigung* or Defense of the Land, meaning military transport). The Traffic Division dealt with financial matters, E 2 with operational considerations, and L with military priorities. Within E 2, the following breakdown should be of interest:[6]

Table 1.1. Eisenbahn Operations Division

E 2 (Operations)	Max Leibbrand (from 1942: Gustav Dilli)
21 (Passenger Trains)	Paul Schnell
211 (Special Trains)	Otto Stange

Stange administered the transport of Jewish deportees. He received the requests for trains from Adolf Eichmann's office in the Security Police and channeled them to financial and operational offices in the Reichsbahn.[7] The position and designation of 211 on the organization chart point to two important features of the deportation process. The first is that the Jewish deportees were always booked as people, even though they were carried in box cars. The passenger concept was essential in order that the Reichsbahn could collect the fare for each deported Jew in accordance with applicable tariffs and to preserve internal prerogatives and divisions of jurisdiction—the passenger specialists would remain in control. The second characteristic of Stange's office is indicated by the word "special." He dealt only with group transports, each of which had to be planned.

Passenger trains were either regular (*Regelzüge*), moving at hours stated in published schedules, or special (*Sonderzüge*), assembled and dispatched upon demand. Jews were deported in *Sonderzüge* and the procurement and scheduling of such trains was a lengthy and involved procedure that had to be administered at the regional level, particularly in the Generalbetriebsleitung Ost (General Directorate East), one of three such *Leitungen* in Nazi Germany. Ost was concerned with trains directed to Poland and occupied areas farther to the east, and hence Jewish transports from large parts of Europe were channeled through this office. An abbreviated chart of the Generalbetriebsleitung would look as follows:[8]

Table 1.2. General Directorate East of the Reichsbahn

Generalbetriebsleitung Ost	Ernst Emrich
I. Operations	Eggert (Mangold)
L	Bebenroth
P (Passenger Schedules)	Fröhlich
PW (Passenger Cars)	Jacobi
II. Traffic	Simon (Hartmann)
III. Main Car Allocation Office for Freight Cars	Schultz

In this array of officials, it was primarily Wilhelm Fröhlich and Karl Jacobi who dealt with Jewish train movements. Conferences were called and dates were fixed for transport programs aggregating forty or fifty trains at a time: ethnic Germans, Hitler Youth, laborers, Jews—all were on the same agenda.[9] The actual schedules were written locally, in the Reichsbahndirektionen, or in the Generaldirektion der Ostbahn, the railway network in central Poland that dispatched Jews on short hauls from ghettos to death camps nearby.[10] The Reichsbahndirektionen were also responsible for the allocations of cars and locomotives. Only then were transports assembled for the Jews loaded, sealed, dispatched, emptied, and cleaned, to be filled with new, perhaps altogether different cargoes, in the circulatory flow. The trains moved slowly and most were overloaded. The norm in Western Europe or Germany was a thousand persons per train.[11] During 1944, transports with Hungarian Jews averaged three thousand.[12] In Poland, such numbers were often exceeded. One train, fifty cars long, carried 8,205 Jews from Kolomea to the death camp of Bełżec.[13] Unheated in the winter, stifling in the summer, the cars, filled with men, women, and children, were death traps in themselves. Seldom would a transport arrive without 1 or 2 percent of the deportees having died en route.

One thinks of railroads as providing a service. What they produce is "place utility," and in this case, they contributed their industriousness and ingenuity to the possibility of annihilating people, by the thousands at a time, in places where gas chambers had been installed. The Order Police, like the Reichsbahn a major apparatus of the Third Reich, was also needed over a long period of time in a wide geographic area, and its utility manifested itself in several stages of the destruction process, from concentration to killings.

Case II: The Indispensability of the Order Police

Nazi Germany was in essence a "police state," a type of regime that implies limitless power over the population. Under Heinrich Himmler, the offices and units of the SS and Order Police were welded into an organization that was a symbol of much that Nazism stood for: arrests and concentration camps, racism and destruction. The police components of this power structure were grouped under two main offices: Security Police, directed by Reinhard Heydrich, and Order Police, commanded by Kurt Daluege, organized thusly:[14]

Table 1.3. Security Police (Sicherheitspolizei, Sipo)

Gestapo, ca. 40,000 to 50,000 men

Criminal Police (Kripo), ca. 15,000

Table 1.4. Order Police (Ordnungspolizei, Orpo)

Stationary (Einzeldienst), ca. 250,000, including reservists
    Cities: Schutzpolizei (Schupo)
    Rural: Gendarmerie

Units (battalions and regiments), ca. 50,000, including reservists

Indigenous personnel in occupied territory of the USSR:
    Schutzmannschaft (Schuma), ca. 100,000, including Einzeldienst and
    Schuma battalions

Other offices (technical services, volunteer fire departments, etc.)

Comparing the Security Police and the Order Police, we may note two differences between them. The Security Police, in which the Gestapo was the predominant element, could be regarded as a new institution, whereas the conventional Order Police was old and established in Germany. Security Police—spread out over a continent—were relatively few; Order Police were clearly more numerous. Even so, the Ordnungspolizei was strained by the extent and variety of its assignments.

The Einzeldienst, a term denoting stationary duty that could be performed by a single individual, was significant mainly in the Reich and annexed territories, while mobile formations (battalions and regiments) were important primarily outside of home or incorporated regions. In most of the occupied countries, including France and the General Government of Poland, where German Order Police personnel served only in units, an indigenous police force remained in place to carry out its own tasks and to assist the Germans in theirs.

The areas wrested from the USSR were covered by a thin layer of Order Police, composed of both Einzeldienst and units. Einzeldienst, stationed in large urban centers as well as in many rural zones, reached a total of close to fifteen thousand at the end of 1942; battalions not fighting at the front contained a similar number of men.[15] To augment this German police establishment, a native Schutzmannschaft was created that by 1 July 1942 had already grown to 42,708 in Einzeldienst within cities and on the land, and to 33,270 in Schuma battalions.[16] The so-called rural districts in Latvian, Lithuanian, White Russian, and Ukrainian regions included small towns with many Jewish residents as well as villages with purely Baltic or Slavic populations. Such a district (*Gebiet*), generally with around 250,000 inhabitants, was garrisoned by a German Gendarmerie platoon and its native helpers. The fairly typical rural *Gebiet* of Brest-Litovsk in the occupied Ukraine was controlled by twenty-six Gendarmerie men (fifteen of them older reservists) and 308 Ukrainian Schuma.[17] If all of these figures appear to be small, they should be juxtaposed with the numerical strength of the Security Police. Gestapo and Criminal Police in the entire occupied USSR were barely a few thousand, and when a Security Police post was placed in a rural area, it would contain around a half dozen men.

The sheer geographic expanse of the Order Police is in fact the principal clue to its function in destructive operations. The Orpo was the ever-present standby force that could be drawn upon whenever Jews had to be concentrated or killed. In Amsterdam, Order Police contingents were needed to round up Jews for deportation.[18] In eastern Europe, Order Police guards were posted near the walls and at the gates of ghettos. For example, in Warsaw, a company of a police battalion was steadily engaged in ghetto supervision.[19] Similarly, in Riga, eighty-eight Schuma were assigned to this duty.[20] And so on, for hundreds of ghettos. Order Police detachments were also guarding laborers outdoors. One Order Police battalion and seven Schuma battalions were deployed along Durchgangsstrasse IV, a thousand-kilometer road construction project from the Danube estuary to Taganrog, on which many Jews worked and died.[21] Furthermore, Order Police routinely accompanied the special trains to their destinations.[22] To put it simply, what the victim saw from a ghetto fence, a labor camp, or a boxcar, were the rifles of ordinary policemen.

The Order Police could not be dispensed with in killing operations themselves. A police battalion (the 9th in 1941 and the 3rd in 1942) was divided among the four Einstatzgruppen of the Security Police that followed the German armies into the USSR to shoot Jews and Communists.[23] Two Order Police detachments in Kiev assisted Einsatzkommando 4a of Einsatzgruppe C in the massacre of Babi Yar.[24] An Order Police contingent was similarly engaged in herding Jews to shooting sites near Riga.[25] A Lithuanian Schuma battalion was stationed in Maidanek,[26] and German Order Police from Łódz were transferred to the death camp at Chełmno (Kulmhof).[27] Often, officers of the Order Police were all but in charge of the killings. During the summer of 1942, when an attempt was made to annihilate the Jews in each of several dozen rural *Gebiete* of the occupied USSR, the local Gendarmeriefu̅hrer, deploying his Germans and native helpers, would surround a small-town ghetto with guards standing approximately twenty meters apart, round up the Jews inside, and supervise the shootings in ditches nearby.[28] To the west of the USSR, in the improvised killing centers of the General Government, Order Police personnel with previous experience in euthanasia operations were serving not only as guards, but also in command. Such was the career of Franz Stangl, commander of Sobibór and, thereafter, Treblinka.[29]

To be sure, neither the railroads nor the Order Police fit any preconceived notion of an ideological vanguard. For that very reason, however, their heavy participation in relentless acts of mass destruction should engage our attention. If nothing else, this history should tell us that if an Adolf Hitler and his Nazi movement of party offices and SS formations were essential for the destruction of the Jews, so was at least in equal measure the readiness—in the fullest sense of the word—of ordinary agencies to engage in the extraordinary tasks inherent in the Final Solution.

Bureaucratic Preparedness

The all-encompassing readiness for action of the diverse machinery of public and private agencies is one of the key phenomena of the bureaucratic destruction process. It resulted, in the case of several professions, in complete reversals of time-honored roles. An obvious example is furnished by the physicians who performed medical experiments in camps; or who, as public-health officials, urged the creation of hermetically sealed ghettos for the ostensible purpose of preventing the spread of typhus from Jewish inhabitants to the surrounding population; or who, as specialists in psychiatry, administered the euthanasia program, which was transformed in the General Government into a network of camps to kill approximately 1.5 million Polish Jews. Indeed, one of the euthanasia physicians, Dr. Irmfried

Eberl, was the first commander of Treblinka.[30] A second illustration of such negation is the planning by offices labeled "Population and Welfare" of deportations of ghetto Jews to death camps.[31] Yet a third instance of goal transformation may be glimpsed in the efforts of civil engineers or architects to construct the ultimate antithesis of a shelter or home—the concentration camp, especially the installations designed for controlled, efficient mass annihilation.[32]

What prompted such a sprawling bureaucratic machine to involve itself so profoundly in a single direction toward death and more death? There were, of course, leaders who gave orders, for this was, after all, the state that utilized the *Führerprinzip*, the leadership principle. Clearly, if orders had been disregarded or evaded, the destruction of the Jews could not have been carried out.[33] Scarcely less important, however, is the fact that the process could not have been brought to its conclusion if everyone would have had to wait for instructions. Nothing was so crucial as the requirement that the bureaucrat had to understand opportunities and "necessities," that he should act in accordance with perceived imperatives, and most especially so when it was not easy to enunciate them in plainly written words. The German historian Uwe Adam has shown that, already before the war, there was a pronounced tendency to dispense with laws and other formal enactments. Laws (*Gesetze*) most especially were to be held to a minimum. "Implementary decrees" no longer carried into effect the laws to which they referred and, like the 11th Ordinance to the Reich Citizenship Law, which dealt with confiscations, contained entirely new subject matter.[34] Decree-making gave way to government by announcement, as in the case of a Heinrich Himmler order of December 1938 to deprive Jews of their driver's licenses, which was published in newspapers directly, without first appearing in the appropriate legal gazette.[35] This administrative evolution continued with more and more reliance on internal directives, first written, then oral. An order by Hitler to annihilate European Jewry was almost certainly given only in oral form.[36] In the final phases, not even orders were needed. Everyone knew what had to be done, and no one was in doubt about directions or goals.

The bureaucracy itself was the source of much that was to transpire. Ideas and initiatives were developed by experts in its ranks. They were submitted as proposals to supervisors and returned as authorizations to their originators. The foremost example is the famous Göring directive at the end of July 1941 charging Heydrich with organizing the "final solution of the Jewish question" in Europe.[37] It was drafted by Eichmann at the request of Heydrich and presented to Göring ready for signature (*unterschriftsfertig*).[38] Every word, including an opening reference to an earlier directive for expediting Jewish emigration, was carefully chosen. The substantive paragraph, with its euphemism about a final solution, was designed to assure the necessary backing for maximum freedom of action.

Not surprisingly, a constant reliance on bureaucratic initiation eventually brought about the existence of experts accustomed to dealing with Jewish matters in particular. Many agencies had one or more of these specialists: Lösener and Globke in the Interior Ministry, Mädel in the Finance Ministry, Rademacher in the Foreign Office, Wetzel in the Ministry for the Occupied Eastern Territories, Stange in the Reichsbahn, Eichmann in the Security Police. This kind of specialization emerged also in the field. The organization chart of the Finance Office of the Reichskommissar in the Ostland shows an official assigned to Jewish property.[39]

Occasionally, there were enthusiasts who were not constantly preoccupied with Jewish matters in the normal course of their activities, but who would not relinquish an opportunity to go out of their way to leave their imprint on the annihilation process. One of these men was the army's Major General Otto Kohl who, until 15 June 1942, was in charge of transport, civilian, and military, in the occupied zone of France.[40] On 13 May 1942, he received an SS captain, the deportation specialist Theodor Dannecker, for an hour and a half, to assure him: "When you tell me 'I want to transport ten thousand or twenty thousand Jews from France to the East,' you can count on me to provide the necessary rolling stock and locomotives." Kohl explained that he regarded the rapid solution of the Jewish question in France as a vital necessity for the army of occupation, and that therefore he would always maintain a radical point of view, even if some people might regard him as "raw."[41] Most participants, however, were aware of the fine line between volunteering one's services, as Kohl had done, and acting, when the time came, in the full use of one's office. Although they avoided an appearance of rawness or reality, they did not have to be goaded to destroy human lives.

Viewing the makeup of the administrative machine as a whole, we must conclude that there was very little prodding or purging of the German bureaucracy. The Reichsbahn or the Order Police could hardly have been pressured in any case. No one but a railroad man could dispatch a train, and no one but the Schutzpolizei and the Gendarmerie could provide police garrisons in the farthest corners of Europe. Within the entire system, internal directives were, if anything, few and sparse. The fact is that the initiators, formulators, and expediters, who at critical junctures moved the bureaucratic machine from one point to the next, came from within that apparatus. Overburdened as they often were, they contributed their share to the destruction of the Jews as a matter of course.

The Preservation of Procedures

Even as the bureaucracy of annihilation consisted in large part of regular personnel in well-established agencies, so the methods of destruction were to a great extent the traditional means of administrative action. Normal procedures were employed in abnormal situations, as if extreme decisions were not being made, and there were no discernible differences between everyday government functions and the Final Solution.

Let us take the example of setting up a concentration camp. When Auschwitz was being expanded, condemnation proceedings were launched to acquire public and private property with a view to bringing about land transfers,[42] and when barracks were being built and cyanide gas was being procured, the acquisition of materials was subject to the allocation mechanisms of Albert Speer's Ministry for Armaments.[43]

The routines were being followed with even greater perseverance in financial matters. Fiscal integrity was not to be impaired in the destruction process. Once, Heinrich Himmler himself had to consider the case of an SS lieutenant who in a previous role as a "trustee" of real estate had been obliged to manage the property for the benefit of the Reich until it could be sold to a new owner but who had "prematurely" terminated leases of Jewish tenants with resulting losses of rent. Had the officer violated his fiduciary responsibility?[44]

A larger quandary faced the German municipal officials of Warsaw after the sudden mass deportations of the ghetto's Jews had begun in July 1942. Utility bills for electricity and gas had not been paid, and how was this debt going to be covered?[45] A similar dilemma was generated for the chief of the Finance Division of the Generalkommissariat Latvia (Dr. Neuendorff) who discovered that taxes owed by dead Jews could not be collected without transfer to his office of money realized from disposals of their confiscated property.[46]

One of the biggest problems was the financing of transport. The Reichsbahn derived its income from clients, that is, people, corporations, or agencies requiring space on its equipment for personal travel or for shipments of cargo. The client for a death train was the Gestapo and the travelers were Jews. The fare, payable by Gestapo offices, was calculated at the passenger rate, third-class, for the number of track kilometers, one way only, with reductions for children. For guards, the round trip price was charged.[47] If at least four hundred Jews were deported, group rates were applicable.[48] Arrangements could be made directly or through the official travel bureau (Mitteleuropäisches Reisebüro).[49] The Gestapo, however, had no budget for transport and it would have been awkward to present a bill for the deportations to the Finance Ministry. Accordingly, a policy of "self-financing" was instituted whereby the funding burden was shifted to authorities in foreign areas where Jewish property had been expropriated or to Jewish communities themselves. In the satellite state of Slovakia, for example, the Foreign Office argued that the Slovak government should pay for the "resettlement," and that, in exchange, the Jews would not be returned.[50] In Germany, the Gestapo directed the official Jewish community organization, the Reichsvereinigung der Juden in Deutschland, to collect cash "contributions" from deportees at the point of their departure to help defray the costs of their future existence in the "east."[51] Such levies were deposited in special accounts "W" that the Gestapo could control. The Finance Ministry, which discovered the stratagem, considered it an evasion of the basic principle that only the ministry could collect funds for the Reich and disburse them to agencies as needed, but it acquiesced in the practice.[52] Even more complex was the payment for transports leaving Holland or France, Italy or Greece, for Auschwitz. These trains passed not only through various countries, but also through several currency zones, and in this traversal the balance of payments had to be considered every time a border was crossed.[53] So costly and difficult were all of these funding requirements that at one point consideration was given to the possible erection of a death camp in western Germany for Jews from western countries.[54]

"Self-financing" was involved also for projects other than transport, such as the building of the Warsaw ghetto wall. The chairman of the ghetto's Jewish council, Adam Czerniakow, protested to the German ghetto commissar against this burden on the community's treasury, arguing that since the ghetto had been created for the stated purpose of protecting the non-Jewish population from the spread of epidemics, the assessment was tantamount to asking the pharmacist to pay the bill for the medicine.[55]

The legal procedures and accounting routines were the essential tools of a decentralized apparatus that was attempting to preserve non-Jewish rights at every turn and to balance the books at all times. By these means, the bureaucrat would satisfy himself that his actions were appropriate and proper. He could equate correctness with rightness and accuracy with accountability. The culmination of this way of thinking may be observed in the reporting system, particularly the regular flow of daily, monthly, or annual reports from regional or local offices. Just as there were no special agencies or extraordinary operating funds for the destruction of the Jews, so there was no separate reporting channel or segregated record-keeping in matters of annihilation.[56] Frequently, offices and units in the field would therefore make references to the Final Solution only in long summaries of diverse activities. Such reports, with their markings denoting authorship and distribution, followed a rigid format, maintained a single perspective, and were cast in a laconic, matter-of-fact style. Typical is a sentence from the war diary of the Armament Inspectorate in the Netherlands for November 1942: "The accelerated implementation of the de-Jewification action by the commander of the Security Police is being accompanied by unavoidable disturbances in fur and clothing enterprises under contract with the armed forces."[57]

For many of these officials, the Jews became a subheading. We see it in rubrics: Wages—Jews, Rations—Jews, Taxes—Jews, Production—Jews. The Jews are absorbed in the daily passage of events, and there is seldom any disconcerting emphasis on their ultimate fate.

Even secrecy could be abandoned in record management. Railroad timetable orders were being dispatched without stamps calling attention to their sensitivity,[58] and in Riga a bureaucrat noted in 1942 that correspondence about the Jewish "estate" (*Nachlass*) in the Trusteeship Division of the German administration of Latvia was no longer classified for security purposes.[59] In a sense, nonlabeling became the ultimate camouflage.

The Perpetrator

What sort of man then was the perpetrator? The very structure and practices of the German bureaucracy should provide us with indications of his character. He valued his competence and efficiency, surmounting innumerable obstacles and adverse conditions. He knew what to do without having to ask for directives. Political platforms and campaigns provide little specific content for bureaucratic action, and Nazi Germany was no different in this respect. The public utterances of leaders and propagandists, the flags, torches, and drums, all these were acts of psychological mobilization that gave theme, form, and pace to the physical measures that were to follow. The bureaucrat, however, was not a creation of the Nazi Party, nor was he an old-fashioned indoctrinated antisemite. Julius Streicher's *Der Stürmer* was not his literature. When the war ended, he would assert that he had never hated Jews, and in any nineteenth-century sense, he did not harbor such feelings in actual fact. He had stood above the small issues to face the larger challenge, though he would not talk in such terms any more than he would have written the word "kill" in an order or report.

Some observers have already recognized that the diffuse machine that destroyed the Jews was staffed by people who would not be recognized for what they were if one talked to them in a living room or some other quiet place. Their social mores were not atypical and their family life and personal concerns were completely commonplace. To one commentator this was "banality." Another, noting the rote manner of bureaucratic action, may find that the most salient trait of German officialdom was a kind of stupefaction, a vast indifference to the nature and consequence of one's acts. Yet we must beware of veneers. There is nothing that appears banal in Eichmann and his many colleagues as soon as they are seen in their acts of destruction. Nor can we describe them as robots when we recall how they deliberated about definitions and classifications, gains and costs. To be sure, they left unsaid much that they thought, for they were breaking barriers and crossing thresholds in ways that bureaucrats seldom attempt. What they did was designed to make history and they were aware of their roles in this undertaking. In the basement of the Nuremberg Traffic Museum, secluded from the gaze of casual visitors, there is a railway map. It shows the network of lines under German control in 1942, the year of its greatest extent.

Notes

1. These four hierarchical structures and their roles as independently operating conglomerates were first recognized by Franz Neumann, *Behemoth* (New York: Oxford University Press, 1942), 467–70. The US prosecution at Nürnberg classified its evidentiary material under four headings: NG, NOKW, NO, and NI, corresponding to the four groups identified by Neumann.

2. Negotiations (by the Foreign Office and SS representatives attached to German embassies and legations) were conducted with Vichy France, Italy, Croatia, Slovakia, Bulgaria, Romania, and Hungary, not always successfully. For characteristic criticism of a Slovak law defining the term "Jew," see *Donauzeitung* (Belgrade), 10 December 1941, 3.

3. Dokumentationsdienst der DB, *Dokumentarische Enzyklopädie V—Eisenbahn und Eisenbahner zwischen 1941 und 1945* (Frankfurt am Main: Redactor Verlag, 1973), 110.

4. Eugen Kreidler, *Die Eisenbahnen im Machtbereich der Achsenmächte während des Zweiten Weltkrieges* (Göttingen: Musterschmidt Verlag, 1975), 278–89.

5. Ibid., 205–6. Albert Speer, *Inside the Third Reich* (New York: Macmillan, 1970), 222–25. Prosecution at Düsseldorf to Landgericht Düsseldorf, 16 March 1970, transmitting indictment of Ganzenmüller, File No. 3 Js 430/67, in Zentrale Stelle der Landesjustizverwaltungen, Ludwigsburg, and in Landgericht Düsseldorf. Statement and answers to questions by Ganzenmüller, 7 October 1964, Case Ganzenmüller, 5:216–27.

6. See the annual *Verzeichnis der obersten Reichsbahnbeamten*, particularly for 1941 and 1943.

7. Statement by Franz Novak, 19 October 1966, Strafsache gegen Novak 1416/ 61, Landesgericht für Strafsachen Wien, 16:33.

8. See *Verzeichnis* and an undated statement by Philipp Mangold, Verkehrsarchiv Nürnberg, collection Sarter, folder aa. Generalbetriebsleitung West was involved in processing transports from France, Belgium, and Holland. Leibbrand to West, Ost, Wehrmachtverkehrsdirektionen Paris and Brussels, Plenipotentiary in Utrecht, and Reichsbahndirektion Oppeln (arrival jurisdiction for Auschwitz), 23 June 1942, Case Ganzenmüller, vol. 4, pt. 3, p. 57.

9. Directives by Jacobi, 8 August 1942 and 16 January 1943, Institut für Zeitgeschichte, Munich, Fb 35/2, 217 and 206.

10. For example, Reichsbahndirektion Königsberg, timetable instruction no. 62, 13 July 1942, 260, and Generaldirektion der Ostbahn, timetable instruction no. 567, 26 March 1943, Zentrale Stelle Ludwigsburg, Polen 167, Film 6, 192–93.

11. Summary of Reich Main Security Office IV B 4 conference in Düsseldorf, under chairmanship of Eichmann, March 1942, Case Novak, 17:203–7.

12. Report by Lt. Col. Ferenczy (Hungarian gendarmerie), 9 July 1944, Case Novak, 12:427.

13. Reserve lieutenant of Schutzpolizei (Wessermann?) to Kommandeur of Ordnungspolizei for Galician district in Lwów, 14 September 1942, Zentrale Stelle Ludwigsburg, USSR, 410:508–10. About two hundred of the Jews were dead on arrival. [See Document E.3 in this book; the lieutenant's name was Westermann and the number of Jews dead on arrival was two thousand—eds.]

14. Affidavit by Walter Schellenberg (Security Police), 21 November 1945, Nuremberg document PS-3033. Kurt Daluege (chief of Order Police) to Karl Wolff (chief of Himmler's personal staff), 28 February 1943, Nuremberg document NO-2861. Daluege was the only Order Police general who began his career in the SS.

15. Daluege to Wolff, 28 February 1943, NO-2861.

16. Order Police strength report (Stärkenachweisung) of Schuma for 1 July 1942, Bundesarchiv R 19/266. Firemen and auxiliaries not included in the figures. Year-end data given by Daluege to Wolff, 28 February 1943, NO-2861. By December, the Schuma (without firemen or auxiliaries) was well over a hundred thousand.

17. Gendarmeriegebietsführer in Brest-Litovsk (Lt. Deuerlein) to Kommandeur of Gendarmerie in Lutsk, 6 October 1942. National Archives microfilm T 454, roll 102.

18. SS Sturmbannführer Zöpf to Judenlager Westerbork, 10 May 1943, Israel Police Eichmann trial document 590. Otto Bene to Foreign Office, 25 June 1943, NG-2631.

19. The 304th Battalion, replaced in 1941 by the 61st. Zentrale Stelle, Ludwigsburg, Polen 365 d and e, passim.

20. Instructions by Captain Kampa, 22 June 1942, National Archives microfilm T 459, roll 21. The original force was larger. Instructions by Major of Schutzpolizei Quasbarth, 24 April 1942, National Archives microfilm T 459, roll 21. The men belonged to the 20th Latvian (Guard) Battalion.

21. The German battalion was set up in Berlin for this purpose. Schuma included the 4th, 7th, and 8th Lithuanian battalions, the 17th, 23rd, 27th, and 28th Latvian battalions. Hans-Joachim Neufeldt, Jürgen Huck, and Georg Tessin, Zur Geschichte der Ordnungspolizei 1936–1945 (Koblenz: Bundesarchiv, 1957), Tessin, 2:51–68, 101–9. Daluege to Wolff, 28 February 1943, NO-2861.

22. Order by Daluege, 24 October 1941, PS-3921.

23. Tessin, Ordnungspolizei, 2:97. Helmut Krausnick and Hans-Heinrich Wilhelm, Die Truppe des Weltanschauungskrieges (Stuttgart: Deutsche Verlagsanstalt, 1981), 146–47.

24. Reich Main Security Office IV A 1 Operational Report USSR no. 101, 2 October 1941, NO-3137.

25. Text of Soviet interrogation of Friedrich Jeckeln (Higher SS and Police Leader in Ostland), 14 and 15 December 1945, Krausnick and Wilhelm, Truppe, 566–70.

26. Strength Report of Schutzmannschaft, 1 July 1942, [Bundesarchive] R 19/266, and FriedrichWilhelm Kruger to Himmler, 7 July 1943, Himmler Files, folder no. 94, Library of Congress.

27. Adalbert Rückerl, NS-Vernichtungslager (Munich: Deutscher Taschenbuch Verlag, 1977), 262–64.

28. Orchestration of the killings remained in the hands of the Security Police whose representatives would usually appear on the local scene a few days before an operation. See Deuerlein report, 6 October 1942, National Archives microfilm T 454, roll 102. Also,

statement by Zeev Sheinwald (survivor of Luboml, Ukraine), Yad Vashem Oral History document 0-3/2947.

29. Stangl's life was reconstructed in detail by Gitta Sereny, *Into that Darkness* (New York: McGraw-Hill, 1974).

30. On Eberl, see Sereny, *Darkness*, 77, 85, 86, and 160, and Lothar Gruchmann, "Euthanasie und Justiz in Dritten Reich," *Vierteljahrshefte für Zeitgeschichte* 20 (1972): 250.

31. See, for example, report by Richard Turk (Population and Welfare Division, Lublin District) for March 1942, Jüdisches Historisches Institut Warschau, *Faschismus-Getto-Massenmord* (Berlin: Rutten & Loening, 1960), 272–73.

32. Note the career of the architect Walter Dejaco. See Friedrich Brill, "Sie hatten nichts gewusst!" *Aufbau* (New York), 17 March 1962, 5. Dejaco was a body disposal expert in Auschwitz. Report by Untersturmführer Dejaco, 17 September 1942, NO-4467.

33. One of the most telling examples is the attitude of Italian officials and army officers. See Daniel Carpi, "The Rescue of Jews in the Italian Zone of Occupied Croatia" (with documents), *Rescue Attempts during the Holocaust: Proceedings of the Second Yad Vashem International Historical Conference, Jerusalem, 8–11 April 1974*, ed. Israel Gutman and Efraim Zuroff, *Rescue Attempts during the Holocaust* (Jerusalem: Yad Vashem, 1977), 465–525.

34. Uwe Dietrich Adam, *Judenpolitik im Dritten Reich*, Tübinger Schriften zur Sozial- und Zeitgeschichte I (Düsseldorf: Droste Verlag, 1972), esp. 108–13, 240–46, 292–302.

35. Order dated 5 December 1938, in *Völkischer Beobachter*, PS-2682. Also Adam, *Judenpolitik*, 213, 244.

36. The issuance of an oral order from Hitler to Himmler is reported by Eichmann in his autobiography, *Ich, Adolf Eichmann* (Leoni am Stamberger See: Druffel-Verlag, 1980), 176–79, 229–31. See also affidavit by Albert Speer, 15 June 1977, facsimile in Arthur Suzman and Denis Diamond, *Six Million Did Die: The Truth Shall Prevail* (Johannesburg: South African Jewish Board of Deputies, 1977), 109–12.

37. Göring to Heydrich, 31 July 1941, PS-710.

38. Eichmann, *Ich*, 479.

39. Organization plan of Reichskommissar Ostland II (Finance), 17 August 1942, National Archives microfilm T 459, roll 2. His deputy was Bruns.

40. Hans Umbreit, *Der Militärbefehlshaber in Frankreich 1940–1942* (Boppard am Rhein: Harald Boldt Verlag, 1968), 243–44. On that date, the Reichsbahn took over civilian traffic. Directive of Transport Minister (Dorpmüller), 13 June 1942, in Kreidler, *Eisenbahnen*, 356–57.

41. Text in Serge Klarsfeld, ed., *Die Endlösung der Judenfrage in Frankreich* (Paris: Dokumentationszentrum für Jüdische Zeitgeschichte CDJC Paris, 1977), 36–37.

42. Land transfer conferences, 3 November and 17–18 December 1942, under chairmanship of Oberfinanzpräsident Dr. Casdorf, PS-1643.

43. Speer to Himmler, 5 April 1943, Himmler Files, folder no. 67. On gas, see affidavit by Dr. Gerhard Peters, 16 October 1947, NI-9113, and testimony by Joachim Mrugowski, Nuremberg doctors case (*U.S. v. Brand*), transcript 5403-4.

44. Correspondence in National Archives microfilm T 175, roll 60.

45. Durrfeld (*Dezernat* 3 of German city administration in Warsaw) to SS and Police Leader von Sammern, 10 August 1942, and memorandum by Kunze (*Dezernat* 4), 13 August 1942, Zentrale Stelle Ludwigsburg, Polen 365 d, 275–77.

46. Neuendorff to Generalkommissar/Trusteeship (Kunska), 4 June 1942, National Archives microfilm T 459, roll 21.

47. Deutsche Reichsbahn/Verkehrsamt, Łódź, to Gestapo in city, 19 May 1942, enclosing bill for twelve trains, facsimile in *Faschismus-Getto-Massenmord*, 280–81, and directive of Reichsverkehrsdirektion Minsk, 27 January 1943, Fb. 82/2, among others.

48. Paul Treibe (E 1) to Reichsbahndirektionen, copies to Generaldirektion der Ostbahn, Protectorate railways, and Mitteleuropäisches Reisebüro, 26 July 1941, Case Ganzenmüller, special, vol. 4, pt. 3, pp. 47–55.

49. Reichsbahndirektion Vienna (signed Dr. Bockhonn) to Slovak Transport Ministry,
copies in house and to Dresden, Oppeln, and Mitteleuropäisches Reisebüro, 27 April 1942,
Yad Vashem document M-5/18 (1).

50. Luther (Foreign Office/Division Germany) via Trade Political Division to Staatssekretär Weizsäcker, 29 January 1943, NG-5108. Ludin (German minister in Slovakia) to
Foreign Office, 18 April 1942, NG-4404. Representative of Transport Ministry in Slovakia
to Slovak Transport Ministry, 1 March 1945, M-5/18 (I).

51. Reichsvereinigung directive of 3 December 1941, Israel Police document 738.

52. Mädel to Mayer and Kallenbach (all in Finance Ministry), 14 December 1942, Bundesarchiv R 2/12222.

53. Rau (E 1/17) to High Command of the Army, 1 March 1944, and subsequent correspondence in Bundesarchiv R 2/14133.

54. SS Standartenführer Dr. Siegert (budget specialist in the Reich Main Security
Office) to Finance Ministry, 17 August 1942, Bundesarchiv R 2/12158. The precipitat-
ing factor was the heavy transport cost from France to Auschwitz.

55. Entry by Czerniakow in his diary, 2 December 1941, in Adam Czerniakow, *The
Warsaw Diary of Adam Czerniakow*, ed. Raul Hilberg, Stanislaw Staron, and Josef Kermisz
(Briarcliff Manor, NY: Stein and Day, 1979), 304.

56. In Eichmann's office there were ca. 200,000 open and 30,000–40,000 secret folders.
He states that destruction of the records was ordered at the end of January 1945. Eichmann, *Ich*, 155, 449. On Stange's files, see statement by Reichsbahn specialist Karl Heim,
18 April 1969, Case Ganzenmüller, 18:98–103. By their very nature, such records were
filled with Jewish affairs.

57. Armament Inspectorate Netherlands (Vizeadmiral Reimer), War Diary, summary
for 1942, Wi/IA 5.1. German records located in Alexandria, Virginia, during postwar years.

58. Statement by Erich Richter, 11 June 1969, Case Ganzenmüller, 19:5–12. Interrogation of Walter Stier, 16 March 1963, Case Novak, 16:355–57. Richter and Stier were
Reichsbahn specialists in Kraków.

59. Notation by Kunska (Generalkommissar of Latvia/Trusteeship), 27 June 1942, on
copy of directive from Reichskommissar's Trusteeship Office, 30 April 1942, National Archives microfilm T 459, roll 21.

Bibliography

Adam, Uwe Dietrich. *Judenpolitik im Dritten Reich*. Düsseldorf: Droste Verlag, 1972.

Carpi, Daniel. "The Rescue of Jews in the Italian Zone of Occupied Croatia." *Rescue At-
tempts during the Holocaust: Proceedings of the Second Yad Vashem International Historical
Conference, Jerusalem, 8–11 April 1974*, ed. Israel Gutman and Efraim Zuroff, 465–525.
Jerusalem: Yad Vashem, 1977.

Czerniakow, Adam. *The Warsaw Diary of Adam Czerniakow*, ed. Raul Hilberg, Stanislaw
Staron, and Josef Kermisz. Briarcliff Manor, NY: Stein and Day, 1979.

Dokumentationsdienst der DB. *Dokumentarische Enzyklopädie V—Eisenbahn und Eisenbahner zwischen 1941 und 1945*. Frankfurt am Main: Redactor Verlag, 1973.

Eichmann, Adolf. *Ich, Adolf Eichmann*. Leoni am Stamberger See: Druffel-Verlag, 1980.

Gruchmann, Lothar. "Euthanasie und Justiz in Dritten Reich." *Vierteljahrshefte für Zeitgeschichte* 20 (1972): 235–79.

Jüdisches Historisches Institut Warschau. *Faschismus-Getto-Massenmord*. Berlin: Rütten & Loening, 1960.

Klarsfeld, Serge, ed. *Die Endlösung der Judenfrage in Frankreich*. Paris: Dokumentationszentrum für Jüdische Zeitgeschichte CDJC Paris, 1977.

Krausnick, Helmut, and Hans-Heinrich Wilhelm. *Die Truppe des Weltanschauungskrieges*. Stuttgart: Deutsche Verlagsanstalt, 1981.

Kreidler, Eugen. *Die Eisenbahnen im Machtbereich der Achsenmächte während des Zweiten Weltkrieges*. Göttingen: Musterschmidt Verlag, 1975.

Neufeldt, Hans-Joachim, Jürgen Huck, and Georg Tessin. *Zur Geschichte der Ordnungspolizei 1936–1945*. Koblenz: Bundesarchiv, 1957.

Neumann, Franz. *Behemoth*. New York: Oxford University Press, 1942.

Rückerl, Adalbert. *NS-Vernichtungslager*. Munich: Deutscher Taschenbuch Verlag, 1977.

Sereny, Gitta. *Into that Darkness*. New York: McGraw-Hill, 1974.

Speer, Albert. *Inside the Third Reich*. New York: Macmillan, 1970.

Suzman, Arthur, and Denis Diamond. *Six Million Did Die: The Truth Shall Prevail*. Johannesburg: South African Jewish Board of Deputies, 1977.

Umbreit, Hans. *Der Militärbefehlshaber in Frankreich 1940–1942*. Boppard am Rhein: Harald Boldt Verlag, 1968.

GERMAN RAILROADS/JEWISH SOULS

Raul Hilberg

Why should the student of the Jewish holocaust interest himself in the German railroads? Why the concern with that faceless element in a regime noted for its Gestapo and concentration camps? How can railways be regarded as anything more than physical equipment that was used, when the time came, to transport the Jews from various cities to shooting grounds and gas chambers in eastern Europe?

"The railroads were but a means to an end," a veteran official of the German railways declared emphatically during a private conversation in his office in 1976. Yet to many of the men who made the railways their career, these means were the end. As bureaucrats and technocrats, they worked ceaselessly to increase the capacity of the network for all the transports projected in the German Reich, and to the very end they found purpose in that endeavor. In their hands, the railways became a live organism that acted in concert with Germany's military, industry, or SS to make German history.

Railroads and Totalitarianism

The railroads have been overlooked; and because of this omission, the social scientist has lost an important clue to the nature of totalitarianism and the manner in which it may function. To be sure, it has always been easy to discern in the development of railway transport a major factor in the growth of modern authoritarian government. One could see to what extent armies and police depended on trains to carry out deportations or move prisoners to slave labor camps. In the main, however, railroads have consistently been regarded as tools, resources, and possibly weapons, but hardly as actors in their own right. The Deutsche Reichsbahn, as the German railroads were known before and during the war, is no exception to this view.

Such truncated understanding has its reasons. Two of them may easily be identified: one is a conceptual bias, the other an inordinately frustrating search for necessary facts. Conceptions can be limiting. The sociologist or political scientist has many times shied away from the notion that drastic acts could be practiced relentlessly by men who appeared to be as politically innocuous as they were ideologically inert. In this case, moreover, the investigator is dealing with individuals who were grounded in a tradition that demanded of them an effort to provide a service to anyone. Those men do not seem to possess willfulness, and most theorizing about "dictatorships" is still dominated by the supposition that invariably such regimes consist of usurpers who imposed their will on helpless people. The soldiery, functionaries, and small entrepreneurs are all considered members of a broad mass that is held down, silenced, and oppressed. Too seldom does anyone ask the purely mechanistic question of who was actually carrying out that oppression from one day to the next.

A modern society is specialized. Let us accept as an axiom that a specialist in one field cannot perform the tasks of an expert in another. Whether the contribution of a technician is volunteered or coerced, his skill is absolutely essential. The European Jews could not be destroyed without the participation of the Reichsbahn. For that matter, the specialized talents of trained personnel in such diverse groups as the SS, the Foreign Office, industrial enterprises, or banks were all drawn on at various stages of the destruction process for the implementation of particular steps, each bureaucrat having his turn and each doing his part.

The railroads, however, were involved not on the fringe of the operation, but were indispensable at its core. Year after year they transported millions of Jews to the mysterious "east" where the victims could be annihilated quietly, out of range of peering bystanders and prying cameras. The Reichsbahn carried on, under increasingly difficult conditions, almost without letup.

Need for Documentation

Still, it is not enough to say that an analysis of the Holocaust compels us to believe that the Transport Ministry must have had an active role in the destruction process, for in the absence of at least a few concrete examples we perceive once again only the stations, tracks, and trains; we cannot visualize the officeholders who operated the system. In short, we need documentation; but for more than thirty years there has been a dearth of railway documents about death transports. When we consider how many folders with correspondence about anti-Jewish action were found after the war in the captured buildings of military and civilian institutions, such scarcity of Reichsbahn files is conspicuous.

Part of the material may have been destroyed in wartime bombings; more could have been lost in the confusion of the Nazi collapse and the initial Allied occupation. The authors of several postwar studies of the Reichsbahn mention large gaps in their sources, and it must be remembered that these writers are German railroad men. Nevertheless, we know enough about the sheer volume of records in the German bureaucracy, the multiple copies of orders and reports to official recipients, to wonder what has happened to all the internal Reichsbahn memoranda and telegrams that dealt specifically with Jews.

Figure 2.1 is a simplified diagram showing the history of record holdings in the territory of the present German Federal Republic.[1] No Reichsbahn documents to speak of were assembled by the victorious Allies, and consequently no Reichsbahn items appear in the Nuremberg collections. Among the many hundreds of defendants and witnesses—SS officers, generals, bankers, civil servants, diplomats, and doctors—not one was a railroad man. The very subject of the Reichsbahn was hardly even recognized in the thousands of transcript pages accumulated in the trials.

What about the Reichsbahn itself? What disposition did it make of its own files? A letter written on 16 February 1966 by the West German Transport Ministry to a ranking German prosecutor in Dortmund states in its entirety:

Records of the former Reich Transport Ministry are stored neither at the Federal Transport Ministry nor at the Main Administration of the Federal Rail-

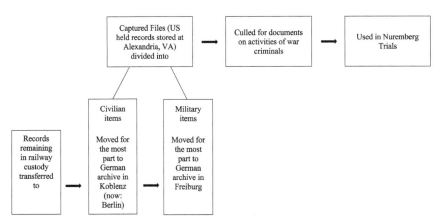

Figure 2.1. History of record holdings in the German Federal Republic

ways. Insofar as they were not lost or destroyed during or after the war, they were transferred to the Federal Archive in Koblenz [now Berlin, eds.]. Based on our information, however, it is hardly likely that you will find materials there on Jewish transports carried out by the previous Deutsche Reichsbahn. I leave it to you whether you want to direct your inquiry to the Federal Archive.[2]

The Transport Ministry was right. Except for a few items of the Reichsbahn correspondence with the SS or the Finance Ministry, there is no evidence on Jewish trains in West Germany's main archive. For all that, the writer of the Transport Ministry letter did not raise the real possibility that significant collections may have been kept in private homes. Various studies, unpublished and published, give indication of such practices. To this day these documents have been shielded from all intruders.[3] West Germany's "brother state," the German Democratic Republic, also has an archive, but it is apparently closed and we cannot be sure how many missing links it may contain.[4] Thus we are confronting an almost complete blackout.

But there are two apertures; one of them is documentary. A few scattered Reichsbahn materials have been found, primarily outside Germany. A single folder containing communications of the railway directorate at Minsk was discovered by Soviet authorities and passed on to German investigators. It describes, in some hundred pages, transports of Jews and other deportees not only to Minsk (where thousands of Jews from Germany were being shot) but also to camps such as Auschwitz. [See Documents C.2 and C.3 in this book.] Here we may glimpse the nature and extent of railway involvement in the destruction of Jewry, though only in fragmentary details. A similar file, more localized in content, was unearthed in Poland; and other stray records—about Düsseldorf, Vienna, France, or Holland—turned up here and there. In all, these items are tantalizingly small openings that reveal only disconnected parts. Not even the most experienced researcher of the Jewish holocaust could reconstruct a coherent picture from such pieces. However, a secondary source base is now available.

The German railroads were investigated by German prosecutors and, although not a single trial has been held in German courts, evidentiary material in the form of compulsory pretrial testimony by former Reichsbahn officials was collected over the years. To the Holocaust student these statements are a kind of secondhand oral history. They are often full of pitfalls, such as critical lapses of memory and utterly misleading "suppositions"; but at the same time, there are quite a few of these depositions, and reading them one may at last attempt that which would otherwise be nearly impossible: a crude description of the actual operations of the Reichsbahn in the destruction of the Jews. We can now say something about the mechanics of these actions and their psychology.[5]

Involvement of the Reichsbahn

The Reichsbahn was one of the largest organizations of the Third Reich. In 1942, its German personnel numbered approximately 1.4 million—close to a half million civil servants and more than 900,000 employees. In addition, the eastern directorates of the network in occupied Poland and Russia employed almost 400,000 indigenous helpers.[6]

Hierarchically, the railways were placed in the Transport Ministry whose chief executive was Julius Dorpmüller. Within the ministry there were two branches, each headed by a Staatssekretär—one for railroads, the other for canal traffic, trucking, and so on. The first railroad Staatssekretär was Wilhelm Kleinmann; his successor in 1942 was Dr. Albert Ganzenmüller, a capable engineer with some Nazi credentials. He was only thirty-seven at the time of his accession, but one should not hasten to assume that he was promoted out of turn only for political reasons. His personnel record had contained the notation "far above average," and his performance during the peak war years bears out that estimate.

Albert Speer asserts that it was he who persuaded Hitler to appoint Ganzenmüller as Staatssekretär. There are in fact several resemblances between Speer and Ganzenmüller. Both were technical men; both rose in power while still young during the war; both were to be confronted with massive problems; and both attempted to meet the challenge head-on. One was concerned with production, the other with transport, and at some point each was drawn into the Jewish holocaust. Speer was tried as a war criminal after the war, although he always sought to disguise his role in the destruction of the Jews. Ganzenmüller, subject to automatic arrest in 1945 because of his high position, was held by the US Third Army. Soon, however, he made his way to Argentina where he functioned as a railway consultant. In 1955, he returned to Germany and served as a transport expert in the German firm Hoesch. He was then investigated by West German authorities and indicted. Retired, he pleads illness now and has not stood trial.[7]

Ganzenmüller was in charge of several railway divisions, three of which are important for our analysis (see Table 2.1).[8] The Traffic Division was client oriented. It produced guidelines for the overall allocation of passenger and freight cars to various civilian users, with an order of preference for designated economic sectors. From time to time, it also set the rates for travel and transport. Operations was responsible for the formation and routing of the trains. This division was concerned with the timetables. Group L (*Landesverteidigung* or Defense of the land) was concerned with the military; it worked on the troop transports and munitions trains ordered by Army High Command/Chief of Transport for all the armed forces.

Every day in the early morning hours a large part of the empty rolling stock was set aside for this utilization.

Table 2.1. Three railway divisions directed by Ganzenmüller

E1	Traffic and Tariff	Treibe (from 1942: Schelp)
E2	Operations	Leibbrand (from 1942: Dilli)
Group L	Armed Forces	Ebeling

Territorially the organization of the railways falls under two headings: Germany itself and the annexed or satellite regions. Within the Reich (including Austria and incorporated territories), we see the structure outlined in Table 2.2. Of the three Generaldirektionen, the eastern was pivotal. A massive stream of traffic was concentrated in movements toward the eastern front, and for our purposes we should keep in mind that most of the deported Jews were also moving in that direction. In fact, Generaldirektion Ost was not only larger than the other two; it also had offices that centralized the operational flow of rolling stock in all directions.

Table 2.2. Railroad structure within Germany

Regional	District	Local
Generaldirektion Ost (Berlin) West (Essen) Süd (Munich)	Reichsbahndirektionen	Railway Stations

Outside the Reich we may distinguish between three forms of authority: direct control of the Reichsbahn, so-called autonomous railroads, and military supervision. The scheme presented in Figure 2.2 is based on the work of the German railway expert Eugen Kreidler,[9] but we must remind ourselves that these tables are formal and rigid; they describe primarily a framework of procedures. The actualities in every case were determined by the gravity of power. In the words of an ordinary freight yard supervisor, "That was a time, after all, when we could move around as we pleased."[10]

It should be noted that the chief of army transport, General Gercke, had two functions in railway operations: he controlled all traffic in some regions through his Wehrmachtverkehrsdirektionen, and he requisitioned military transport in all areas with an organization of continental proportions. This procurement and monitoring network was maintained outside his fiefdoms in Belgrade–Salonika or Bologna for contact with the field representatives of the Reichsbahn's Group L. It underwent some changes over the years and eventuated in several regional Wehrmachttransport-

Under Reichsbahn Control

Generalgouvernement (central Poland)
>   Generaldirektion der Ostbahn (Gedob) in Krakow
>>   German administrative apparatus operationally integrated with Transport Ministry

Occupied USSR
>   Generalverkehrsdirektion Osten in Warsaw
>>   German administrative apparatus operationally integrated with Transport Ministry (initially under a directorate for eastern operations in the office of the chief of Army Transport)

France
>   Hauptverkehrsdirektion in Paris
>>   German administrative layer over French railways (initially Wehrmachtverkehrsdirektion under Chief of Army Transport)

Belgium
>   Hauptverkehrsdirektion in Brussels
>>   German administrative layer over Belgian railways (initially Wehrmachtverkehrsdirektion under Chief of Army Transport)

Netherlands
>   Plenipotentiary of Reichsbahn with Dutch railways in Utrecht

Denmark
>   Plenipotentiary of Reichbahn with Danish railways in Aarhus

"Autonomous" Railroads

"Protectorate" Bohemia-Moravia
>   Plenipotentiary of Reichsbahn (for liaison and directives) in conjunction with Reichsprotektor/Division of Transport over remnant Czech Transport Ministry in Prague

Slovakia
>   Plenipotentiary of Reichsbahn for liaison and directives to Slovak Transport Ministry in Bratislava

Axis Satellites: Hungary, Romania, Bulgaria
>   Reichsbahn Generalvertreter (representatives) in each of the capitals for liaison

Supervised by Chief of Army Transport

Norway
>   Transport Commander over Norwegian railways

Croatia, Serbia, Greece
>   Wehrmachtverkehrsdirektion Südost
>>   An administrative apparatus in Belgrade over indigenous railroads

Italy
>   Wehrmachtverkehrsdirektion in Bologna
>>   Installed after Italian collapse in 1943 over Italian railroads

Figure 2.2. Railroad structure outside Germany

leitungen with headquarters in Berlin, Vienna, Paris, Warsaw, Minsk, and Dnepropetrovsk. As the availability of transport tightened, the Wehrmachttransportleitungen were to acquire increasing importance.

The Reichsbahn reveals a basic differentiation in its central and territorial offices alike. With regard to personnel it was the distinction between the lawyers and accountants on the one hand, and the engineers and mechanical specialists on the other. In functional terms, it was a separation of financial and operation preoccupations. These two work areas became manifest also in the Jewish transports. If we had to state their combined effect in a single sentence we would have to say that the Jews were booked as people and shipped as cattle.

Methods of Payment

In principle, the Reichsbahn was prepared to transport Jews, or any group, for payment. The bill was simply sent to the agency that requisitioned the trains. The amount reflected the number of persons transported and the distance covered. Third-class passenger fare was the base rate. In 1942, this figure was 4 pfennig per track kilometer. Children under ten traveled at half fare; those under four traveled free.[11]

Deportations of Jews began immediately after the conquest of Poland in 1939. The early transports were actually concentration measures—some thousands of Jews were expelled from German cities and incorporated regions to Poland. The requisitioning agency was the SS and Police, specifically the Reich Security Main Office (Security Police and Security Service). The section of the Main Office concerned with "resettlements" was headed by Adolf Eichmann. On 20 February 1941, Eichmann accepted responsibility for the transport costs in the incorporated Polish territories on behalf of the Main Office.[12]

For its part, the Transport Ministry developed a practice that would benefit the Security Police: group fare for deportees. The charge would be half the third-class rate provided that at least four hundred people were being shipped. The minimum amount for a transport was to be 200 Reichsmarks, and no payment was going to be exacted for movements of emptied trains. The Reichsbahn directive, prepared by E 1/15 (Passenger Traffic) and signed by Paul Treibe on 26 July 1941, deals with several categories of "special trains" (*Sonderzüge*) and lists them as shown in Table 2.3.[13] To the financial experts of E 1, it was thus immaterial whether "participants" in travel were voluntary or incarcerated: the privileged ethnic Germans were going to new homes, the hospitalized mental patients to their doom.

Table 2.3. Special trains in the Reichsbahn

Procurement	Participants	Purpose
VOMI (Ethnic German Service Agency)	Ethnic Germans	Resettlement
Gemeinnützige Krankentransport GmbH, Berlin (an "ambulance" service for euthanasia)	Mentally ill people	Removal or evacuation to asylums
Chief of Security Police	Jews and alien persons	Movement out of the German Reich, etc.

The jurisdiction of E 1 was limited to the Greater German Reich, but within that territory it guarded its prerogatives. When Reichsbahndirektion Oppeln wanted to charge for hauling prisoners between Auschwitz and the I. G. Farben track in Dwory on a monthly commuter basis, the ministry asked for data on costs.[14]

While the half-fare rate preceded the heavy deportations of Jews to death camps, it was subsequently applied to such transports as long as they originated in the Reich. In April 1942, the Slovak railways, which had to compensate the Reichsbahn for Jewish *Sonderzüge* traversing German soil on the way to the Generalgouvernement (Poland), asked for the 50 percent reduction. The request, forwarded by Reichsbahndirektion Vienna to the Transport Ministry, was granted.[15] The Slovaks then asked for the same concession from the Ostbahn and again the bill was reduced by half.[16]

The allowance to the Slovaks became a precedent for trains coming from the west. On 14 July 1942, the reduced rate was given to the Jewish *Sonderzüge* in transit from Holland, Belgium, and France—via Aachen, Neuburg, and Neuschanz—to "labor utilization" in Auschwitz. The reduction covered the distance extending eastward from Alsace, and in that area the official Central European Travel Bureau (Mitteleuropäisches Reisebüro GmbH) was designated to process the billing.[17]

Generally the SS attempted to fill a deportation train with one thousand people (two thousand later became the norm).[18] Smaller groups were sometimes transported, in cars attached to regular trains, to a city where a *Sonderzug* was being formed. If a death train contained fewer than four hundred deportees, the SS could report four hundred to take advantage of the special rate.[19]

Not all the routes were affected by the 50 percent fare. There is no indication, for example, of such a policy in the territory of the Minsk directorate. That directorate, however, repeatedly ordered the arrival stations to make separate counts of adults and children under age ten.[20] There was, incidentally, a possibility of surcharges for "exceptional filth" or damage to cars.[21]

Whereas the SS had acknowledged its liability to defray the cost of the transports, it had trouble funding the program. The source of the money was not the regular budget obtained in the usual way from the Finance Ministry, but a complicated shadowy arrangement that was called self-financing. Wherever possible, the Jews themselves were to be the providers of the means with which the transports were procured. Within the borders of prewar Germany, the Jewish Reichsvereinigung was ordered to deposit money in a special account that could be tapped as needed to make payments to the Reichsbahn. Finance Ministry officials discovered the stratagem and almost put an end to it, for it was a violation of the rule that only the ministry could collect and disburse the funds of the state.[22] Within incorporated territory, the German administration of the Łódź ghetto (Gettoverwaltung) was a conduit of payments.[23] For deportations from France, the SS secured the agreement of the German military commander that transportation costs attributable to travel on French soil up to the German border were to be covered from the military occupation budget.[24]

There was evidently no requirement of prepayment, and on occasion, efforts to obtain the money after the fact led to difficulty. During 1944, SS deportation specialists in Holland had ordered by telephone small transports for remaining pockets of Jews from Amsterdam and The Hague to the transit camp Westerbork. When the Nederlandsche Spoorwegen presented statements for the completed service, the SS delayed part of the payment; and the plenipotentiary with the Dutch railways, emphasizing the correctness of the bills, called on the SS to discharge its debt for the balance.[25]

In one case, the Reichsbahn's attempt to collect the fare apparently met with failure. The situation, which arose after the deportation of some 46,000 Jews from Salonika to Auschwitz in the spring of 1943, was complicated in that, as usual, the SS did not have its own funds. Moreover, the required sum had to be furnished in several currencies. The bill amounted to 1,938,488 Reichsmark, and the chief of E 1/17, Ministerialrat Dr. Werner Rau—who was in charge of passenger traffic with foreign countries—himself attended to this delinquency.[26] The correspondence on the Salonika transports, in the files of the Finance Ministry, reveals a lengthy exchange in the following terms.

Normally, whenever one or more currency zones were crossed by the trains, the entire bill was payable to the railroad that was in charge of the first segment of the trip. This organization would act as agent for all the lines responsible for the continuation of the transports—each had to be reimbursed in its own monetary denomination for the distance covered on its tracks. In the specific situation of the deported Greek Jews, the SS wanted the German military commander in Salonika to pay the whole amount from the proceeds of Jewish properties he had confiscated in the area. The military commander, however, only had drachma; occupied Greece was not permitted imports from which he could have built up Reichsmark balances.

Rau was consequently caught in a circular dilemma. The economic attaché with the German Foreign Office mission, Hellmuth Höfinghoff, refused to apply for Finance Ministry permission to allocate Reichsmark to the military commander. The SS reiterated its self-financing principle. The Economy Ministry sided with the SS and at the same time noted that payment was entirely the responsibility of the military. The army quartermaster general agreed that confiscated Jewish property should be attached for this purpose, but insisted that there was no armed forces liability out of its own general funds. In September 1944, the Finance Ministry ruled that all Reichsmarks in Greece had to serve military interests, and deportations of Jews carried out more than a year earlier did not qualify under this criterion.

All our material about rates, billing, and collection is fragmentary, but it permits us to restate the salient ground rules in a few short propositions. The deportation of the Jews was civilian passenger traffic. The client for these transports was the SS. Volume justified substantial rate reductions. The Central European Travel Bureau could handle many of the accounts. And trains could be dispatched before payment was received; in other words, the SS was entitled to credit.

System of Operation

To the Reichsbahn every transport was a business transaction, but financing by itself could not guarantee a train's departure. Germany was at war. Despite some motorization, the German armed forces were heavily dependent on the rails. As the fronts moved farther away from home, there was a problem of stretch-out. Although there was some railway booty, cars as well as locomotives became scarce and, notwithstanding many construction projects, lines were sometimes jammed. The railways were increasingly attacked by bombers and partisans; these attacks interrupted traffic and aggravated shortages. Yet throughout this time Jews were being sent to their deaths.

What transpired with the SS requisitions? How were they processed in the face of competing claims for space? Who determined what was to be done? Jews could not simply be moved in regular passenger trains; the SS wanted sealed transports that had to be assembled from available rolling

stock and dispatched on open tracks. The two ingredients of this requirement were equipment and time—the allocation of cars and construction
of schedules.

Portraying these Reichsbahn operations is not an easy task, but we must
at least attempt to identify the steps that were taken from the initiation
of a transport to its arrival at a camp. Figure 2.3 is a tabular representa-
tion of the process with two variants, one showing the administration of
a transport program from a point in western Germany to Auschwitz (in
incorporated territory), the other describing the communications chain
for a movement of trains from Białystok (incorporated territory under East
Prussian Königsberg) to Treblinka (in the Generalgouvernement).

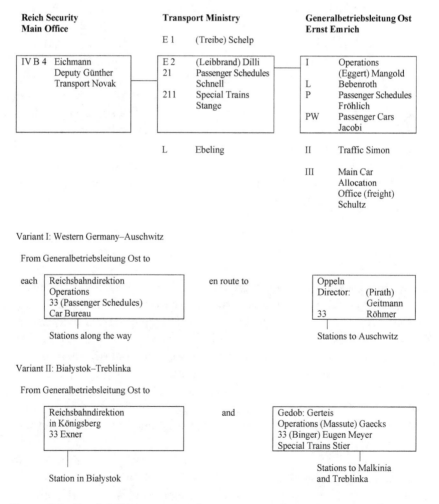

Figure 2.3. Reichsbahn operations from initiation of transport to arrival at camp

A pictorialization of the Reichsbahn shows its asymmetries and dispro-
portions. The numerical designations of offices changes from the ministry
to its territorial apparatus (21 is turned into 33); Group L—separate in
the ministry—becomes part of operations in the three Generalbetriebsleitungen; and only Generalbetriebsleitung Ost has the Main Car Allocation
Office (freight) and section PW (Personenwagen)—the circulation of cars
transporting passengers. In effect, functions were more concentrated in
the field and purposes more emphasized. But then, the very existence of
the Reichsbahn exemplified a tilt in German transportation: the primacy of
ground over air and sea, and of rails over roads and canals. Moreover, in its
wartime mobilization, the Reichsbahn reflected more and more a predom-
inance of traffic patterns: military over civilian, freight over passengers,
east over west.

At the same time, however, old established principles and definitions
were not abandoned in the metamorphoses. Paralleling the financial concept that deportees were travelers, we may note that orders for Jewish
transports were signed by Dr. Karl Jacobi of the passenger car circulation
section as if the substitution of freight cars had no bearing on his responsi-
bilities. Similarly, the Fahrplananordungen containing the detailed timetables of the death trains were prepared by the passenger schedule sections
(33) without regard to the fact that the deportees were being shipped in
freight cars like cattle to slaughter. Here, as in so many other organizations
of the German Reich, there was maximum continuity of jurisdiction as well
as minimum change of personnel. As always, ordinary officials performed
extraordinary tasks.

Transports were initiated in the Reich Security Main Office by Adolf
Eichmann's "resettlement" section. The actual liaison with the railroads
was primarily the job of Franz Novak. If we were to fit him into the Main
Office, we would have to write IV-B-4-a-2, Eichmann being the "4" and
Günther the "a." There were, however, regional contacts as well. Within
Germany itself local Gestapo offices did much of the paperwork in connection with trains originating in their areas. In conquered and allied territories, IV-B-4 had field offices (Paris, Salonika, or Bratislava). Eichmann's
own network did not extend to the Generalgouvernement or regions taken
from the USSR, but there the Main Office's Security Police commanders
might requisition trains as his agents or in pursuance of overall plans negotiated in Berlin.

In our simplified chart of the decision flow, the first link is the Main
Office—Reichsbahn axis. The channel ran from SS Captain Franz Novak
to Amtsrat Otto Stange. Novak would go to Stange's office, but from time
to time he would also see "this one and that one." He brought the requisitions to the ministry and took the complete transport program back to the

Main Office for excerpting and channeling it to the SS and Police network that was engaged in loading, guarding, and unloading the trains.

Stange was a sixty-year-old professional railroad man who was assigned to division E 2 from Group L.[27] To quote Novak, "Stange sat all alone in a small room of the Transport Ministry on Voss Street."[28] A secretary points out that the Amtsrat did not write much and that he used the telephone a great deal.[29] A colleague who observed him closely says that he was withdrawn and "very convinced of the importance of his work and his person." He was "choleric," sick with gallstones, and once hospitalized. Apparently his telephone conversations were conducted in such a loud voice that neighbors requested other offices. The telephone notwithstanding, there was a considerable record file; and Stange's colleague, driven by curiosity, opened some of the folders and read them. The letters received by Stange had an unusual feature: they were addressed to him, a mere Amtsrat, directly.[30] To be sure, the information sent out of his office was disseminated over a wide area.

The first requirement for a transport was a locomotive and cars. How were they allocated? We know that, after 1941, coaches were reserved only for guards; freight cars with doors would do for deportees. In mid-1942, the Reichsbahn possessed about 850,000 cars of all types, and an average of around 130,000 stood empty for loading every day.[31] A large part of that supply was channeled through Group L to the military, and guidelines specifying product categories were worked out by E 1 for the civilian sector.[32]

The ministry, at all events, addressed itself in the main to the large picture. Dr. Fritz Schelp, who took over E 1 in 1942, tells us that resettlement transports were not even included in any all-encompassing scheme since they were numerically insignificant. Considering a total volume of more than 20,000 trains per day, neither his division nor the Main Car Allocation Office (attached to Generalbetriebsleitung Ost) was interested in ten transports or one hundred.[33] Let us not mistake, however, the real meaning of such "negligibility." It implies not an impossibility of performance, but the very opposite. The Reichsbahn moved troops and industrial cargo, soldiers on furlough and vacationers, foreign laborers and Jews. Sometimes space was preempted by the army or some other claimant, but Jewish transports were put together whenever and wherever there was a possibility of forming a train. They too had some priority.

The correspondence of E 2/21 (Schnell) or its section 211 (Stange) has not come to light.[34] We know only that E 2 directives for assigning cars and scheduling trains were routed to the Generalbetriebsleitungen. The orders specified the Leitung that was to take charge of a program and the time frame for its completion.

E 2 issued orders for all requisitions involving five or more special trains. At the beginning of the war, the individual Reichsbahndirektionen were allowed to proceed on their own with one to five *Sonderzüge*, subject only to prior consent of the Main Car Allocation Office and a report to 21. On 14 July 1941, following the assault on the USSR but preceding the operation of death camps, the rule was spelled out further and modified. Now the Direktionen could go ahead only with transports that were "obviously and undoubtedly" essential for the war or maintenance of life. For certain specified contingencies, such as the movement of prisoners to concentration camps or mental patients from asylums, the Direktionen could act also if the purpose was not obviously and undoubtedly vital. Division E 2 continued to reserve jurisdiction for processing requisitions of more than five trains, and it repossessed decision-making power for single transports in a list of categories that included "resettlements of Jews."[35]

The five-train rule was handed down by the "internationally respected" Dr. Max Leibbrand.[36] We have no further documents signed by him except one, dated 23 June 1942, that shows how E 2 exercised its powers. The program in question encompassed a projected transport of 90,000 Jewish victims from France, Belgium, and Holland to Auschwitz. Generalbetriebsleitung Ost/PW was empowered to regulate the allocation of cars with the admonition that as far as possible the western Hauptverkehrsdirektionen were to draw the cars from their own supplies. Generalbetriebsleitung West (in cooperation with Ost) was appointed to set up the schedules with maximum use of available timetables. The goal was six or seven *Sonderzüge*, each containing one thousand persons, per week, starting approximately 13 July. The directive was addressed to Generalbetriebsleitung West, to PW, and L of Ost, the Hauptverkehrsdirektionen in Paris and Brussels, the Plenipotentiary in Utrecht, and the Reichsbahndirektion in Oppeln (whose territory included the Auschwitz railroad station).[37]

Since directives were also sent for special transports of ethnic Germans, agricultural laborers, children, and so on, the Generalbetriebsleitung receiving the orders would hold a conference to draft a "circulatory plan" listing all of the trains by type, date, and places of origin and destination. [See Document C.3 in this book for an example of such a plan.] Such conferences took place in Berlin, Nuremberg, Bamberg, and Frankfurt am Main.[38] For the deportation of the Slovak Jews in 1942 there were joint German-Slovak meetings in Passau and (twice) in Bratislava. A German Foreign Office dispatch lists the German participants in the first of the Bratislava deliberations (approximately 10–15 June 1942).[39] Looking up the positions of these Germans in the railroad directory, we obtain the picture shown in Table 2.4.[40]

Table 2.4. Positions of German participants in the first Bratislava deliberations (ca. 10–15 June 1942)

Reichsbahndirektor Koesters	Chief, GBL Ost/Operations/M (locomotives)
Reichsbahnrat Bebenroth	Chief, GBL Ost/Operations/L
Abteilungspräsident Scharrer	Chief, Gedob/Operations/Locomotives
Oberreichsbahnrat Meyer	Chief, Gedob/Operations/33
Oberreichsbahnrat Röhmer	Chief, RBD Oppeln/Operations/33
SS Captain Novak	IV B 4

The specific involvement of L, whose principal concern was military traffic, has considerable significance. From correspondence of widely separated Direktionen in the field we may observe that final schedules were reported in two instances to P and PW[41] and in two others to L and PW.[42]

Meetings of the Generalbetriebsleitung Ost were sometimes chaired by a Reichsbahnoberinspektor Bruno Klemm.[43] [See Document A.2 in this book.] His position was too low to be noted in the railroad directory. He was the scheduling expert for special trains in Ost and the work sessions that he conducted were attended by comparatively lower-ranking specialists such as Gedob's *Sonderzüge* Schedules Chief Walther Stier or PW's *Sonderzüge* car expert Fähnrich.[44] According to Stier, Klemm always "drove" his colleagues in these lengthy conferences that went on for days. Klemm, along with Jacobi, was "dragged off" by the Russians when the offices of the Generalbetriebsleitung were overrun in the spring of 1945. His precise assignment and authority are now lost in the haze, but two veterans of Ost have indicated that he worked in L.[45]

A Generalbetriebsleitung might take a month preparing a transport plan before passing it on to the Direktionen in the field, where the cars had to be assembled and where the schedules had to be written. The car bureaus of the Direktionen were expected to be as self-sufficient as possible, although the Main Car Allocation Office could transfer surplus cars from one area to make up for shortages in another. Sometimes the deportees had to change trains en route.[46]

Scheduling in the Section 33 offices was also a matter of some improvisation. It should be pointed out in this connection that timetables were either regular—the kind customarily used for ordinary passenger trains— or *Bedarfsfahrpläne* (which specified the times when trains could depart for shippers interested in transportation). The difference is basic: in the schedule for regular trains departures were not tied to demand; in the *Bedarfsfahrpläne* only the time was fixed—the train had to be requisitioned. The principal users of *Bedarfsfahrpläne* were industry and the army; but

when a particular time slot was not needed for vital cargo or military purposes, it could be made available to the SS for deportations of Jews.[47]

Bedarfsfahrpläne were drawn up to cover relatively short distances, but for
key routes the plans of adjacent zones were coordinated to permit through
traffic in a consecutive pattern. Occasionally a Jewish *Sonderzug* could not
be entered in all the *Bedarfsfahrpläne* for such continuous traversal. Even
then, the train could still leave, going part of the way in *Bedarfsfahrpläne*
that were still open and progressing on the preempted segments in a *Sonderplan*—a special schedule devised for movement between trains rolling
ahead and to the rear. We have a timetable for a Jewish *Sonderzug* projected in a combination of these schedules.[48] In case of cancellations or
other interruptions in the traffic flow, there would be a chain of last-minute
modifications. Now the whole multitude of interdependent offices would
attempt to cope with the complications reverberating through the system
sending communications back and forth, some frantically written by hand.

Jewish Transports

The Jewish *Sonderzüge* had a well-defined place in the constellation of
passenger transports. They were specially labeled. The categorization, as
reconstructed from car circulation plans, timetables, and reports is shown
in Figure 2.4. The planners, even at the local level, were always aware of
the trains with which they were dealing. How was that awareness brought
to bear on the movement of the Jewish trains? Specifically, how were
administrative difficulties resolved? And what were the psychological
reactions?

Administratively, Jewish transports posed a set of special requirements,
such as guard forces on trains and spur lines to killing centers; but, in
addition, the *Sonderzüge* were part of the general burden that had to be
distributed over the whole system. The specific needs were actually the
lesser concern. The detailing of guards was decided, after some explora-
tions, by the beginning of the mass transports in 1941: the Order Police—
essentially policemen from the streets—were assigned to this duty.[49] The
laying of tracks to the ramps in front of the gas chambers, along with signal
equipment and the like, was the responsibility of the local Direktion. It
was handled by its construction office out of its own budget.[50] But outside reinforcements and residual resources could not be commandeered
to solve the systemic problem. The Reichsbahn had a chronic shortage
of personnel; there was not enough rolling stock; and at times the lines
were clogged.[51] It is here that the routines were tested and the real choices
made.

Passenger trains

Special trains (Sonderzüge)

Resettlement trains

Transports carrying Jews

Originating outside Poland (Da)

Originating in Poland (P, Kr, or Pj)

Figure 2.4. Constellation of passenger transports

Several expedients were developed to cope with insufficiency. The formal scheme of rank ordering the uses of cars was one of the methods. It was intrinsically incomplete, necessarily complicated, and ultimately inefficient. A large number of empty trains were moving from points where they had been unloaded to stations where they were supposed to take on important cargo.[52] A premium was consequently placed on filling equipment idled or shuttling between assignments. At a conference in Berlin in March 1942, Eichmann mentioned that he had been offered trains which at some point were going to bring foreign laborers and others from the east.[53] [See Document A.1 in this book.] The SS naturally wanted something better than standby status, but it was able to procure space that way.

To save locomotives and to reduce the total number of transports, the trains were lengthened and the cars loaded to the hilt.[54] In the case of Jewish *Sonderzüge*, the norm of one thousand deportees per train could be pushed to two thousand, and for shorter hauls (in Poland) to five thousand. There might have been less than 2 square feet per person.

The very weight of the trains slowed them. The maximum speed for freight trains became approximately 40 miles per hour, for Jewish trains approximately 30. Moreover, circuitous routes were devised to avoid congestion. The Jews, of course, did not have to be rushed to their destination; they were going to be killed there, not used. A Białystok–Auschwitz schedule reveals the pace: twenty-three hours, not counting the boarding.[55] A Düsseldorf–Riga train took up to three days.[56] [See Documents E.1 and F.1 in this book.] Troop trains had the right of way, prolonging trips still more.[57] The sealed cars often did not have enough water for such long journeys, and nothing is so indelible in the memory of German witnesses as crying mothers holding up parched children during stops.[58] The Jews had to endure suffocating stench in the summer or freezing temperatures in winter. A German guard captain on his part complained when his men had to ride in an unheated coach. He had high praise, however, for the Red Cross ladies who handed hot beef soup to the police as the train passed through icy Lithuania.[59]

In severe situations, the railroad could curtail civilian traffic or throttle it altogether. The ban could be imposed for a week or a month and could affect individual routes or a large region. In the spring of 1941, and again in early 1942, section 33 of the Reichsbahndirektion in Vienna reported postponements or cancellations of Jewish transports because of "adverse conditions."[60] A two-week shutdown was instituted in the Generalgouvernement during the latter half of June 1942; but the Higher SS and Police leader in the area, Krüger, negotiated with the Ostbahn's Gerteis for deportation trains to be made available "now and then" despite the stoppage.[61]

The following month, the railway line to the death camp at Sobibór was closed for repairs. It was just the time when Jews by the hundreds of thousands were to be transported from the Warsaw Ghetto to the Sobibór gas chambers. On 16 July, Chief of Himmler's Personal Staff Karl Wolff telephoned Ganzenmüller for help. Years later, under questioning, Ganzenmüller "assumed" that he had referred the matter to Ministerialdirigent Ebeling of Group L for further action with the Gedob. At the time, he reported back to Wolff that the Warsaw Jews were being directed as of 22 July to the newly constructed (killing) center of Treblinka, and that the Security Police in the Generalgouvernement was remaining in constant touch with the Gedob to assure the dispatch of a daily train with five thousand Warsaw Jews to Treblinka, plus another two trains a week—also carrying five thousand Jews each—from Przemysl to the Belżec (death) camp.[62] [See Document B.5 in this book.] Parenthetically we might note that in another postwar account a young specialist in Gedob/33, Erich Richter, quoted a superior as saying that, pursuant to an order from the Transport Ministry, Jewish resettlement trains were to be sent out as soon as they were "announced" by the SS. Richter himself had never seen a written directive to that effect, but he did sign several of the timetables dispatching trains to Treblinka.[63]

We know of yet another interruption. From 15 December 1942 to 15 January 1943, a general shutdown apparently halted all Jewish deportations in the Generalgouvernement and elsewhere as well (Belgium).[64] By 20 January, however, the flow was resumed. Generalbetriebsleitung Ost had never stopped its planning.[65]

Backlog—a measure of the number of trains that, for various reasons, were held back for more than a few hours at the point of departure or that were aborted because of blockages before they could reach their destinations—became a permanent large-scale problem after the spring of 1943.[66] How could the deportations of Jews be continued under such circumstances? In the spring of 1944, Hungary was occupied by the German Army. A new wave of destruction was in the offing, and in the middle of that year a half million Jews were poured into Auschwitz. They arrived from Hungary and also from Slovakia in high-priority transports under the auspices of the German armed forces.

The military was a customer, not a co-manager, of the railroads; but at a minimum, it had to be a factor in Reichsbahn decisions affecting apportionments of space to all users. We have already seen the proximity of military transports and Jewish *Sonderzüge* in the fact that officials of L were handling both. The army was always in the background when SS requests were approved, and by 1944, its passive presence became active.[67]

A meeting called for 4–5 May in the army's Wehrmachttransportleitung Südost at Vienna was going to deal with the entire movement of trains in the southeast. The conference was attended by military officers, Reichsbahn officials, Hungarian and Slovak transport representatives, SS Captain Novak and a deputy, and a Hungarian police officer. The agenda included the whole spectrum of transport requests: beets, foreign laborers, Jews.[68] Four Jewish transports were to be dispatched each day. They were to be made up of approximately forty-five freight cars, German and Hungarian, plus two cars for guards; each train was to carry about three thousand victims with their baggage. Strong locomotives were needed to pull this weight. According to a Hungarian report, 147 transports were sent out from 14 May to 8 July.[69]

Unresolved is the question, repeatedly raised at one of the trial proceedings against Novak, of whether the Jewish trains were being moved with armed forces bills of lading, in quadruplicate, to speed them on their way.[70] There is evidence, however, that in 1944 transports from Slovakia had been processed in this manner. The Slovak Transport Ministry cited the fact in the hope of obtaining the lower military tariff from the Reichsbahn. The German railroad representative replied that the armed forces papers had been issued to expedite the trains, not to save the Slovaks money.[71]

More than 5 million Jews were killed during the destruction process in ghettos, on shooting grounds, and in gas chambers. In the three-year period between October 1941 and October 1944, the Reichsbahn transported more than half of these people to their deaths. Throughout that time, despite difficulties and delays, no Jew was left alive for lack of transport.

The Reichsbahn moved not only the Jewish deportees; it carried belongings of the dead from camps to Germany for distribution to various recipients.[72] The Ostbahn hauled debris from the site of the Warsaw Ghetto battle.[73] In western Europe, confiscated Jewish furniture was collected by a special staff for utilization in the Reich. These bulky items necessitated not fewer than 735 trains.[74] The railroads were producers when they transported Jews or their expropriated property, but occasionally they were con-sumers as well. The Reichsbahn took advantage of forced Jewish labor[75] and it accepted some of the loot, including 1,576 carloads of furniture, for its bombed-out personnel.[76]

Role of the Reichsbahn

Looking back on the Reichsbahn's role in the destruction of the Jews, we should note something about the officials who were involved with this work, the sort of men they were, the manner in which they managed sen-sitive information, the mode in which they carried on. First and foremost, no one resigned, no one protested, and hardly anyone asked for a transfer.[77] There was no hesitancy in the ranks and no pause in the effort. The per-petrators, it should be stressed, were not a particular group of functionaries appointed to such a task. They were traffic or timetable experts, not spe-cialists in Jewish affairs. Their procedures were not specially adapted to the special character of the Jewish transports. No matter whether the purpose was preservation of life or infliction of death, the Reichsbahn made use of the same rules, the same channels, the same forms. Not even the number of participants was consciously restricted, nor was strict secrecy maintained.

Jacobi's directive containing his circulatory plan of 16 January 1943 went to twenty recipients,[78] the timetable for DA 71 (Aachen–Theresien-stadt) to fifty-two,[79] and a schedule for eight DA trains prepared at Minsk was issued in an edition of three hundred.[80] [See Documents C.1 and C.2 in this book.] In the case of troop transports, care was taken to preclude insight on the part of local railroad personnel into ultimate destinations; a station would know only of movements on the tracks for which it was responsible. The DA and Pj trains, on the other hand, were not shielded by segmentation of scheduling information; everyone knew where they were going. Group L and all those concerned with military transports stamped documents "secret."

If there were such classification for Jewish *Sonderzüge*, the records are no longer available; those that survive lack indication of confidentiality. In fact, the Gedob's Erich Richter states flatly that timetables for Jewish "re-settlement" trains were at most designated "nur für den Dienstgebrauch" (restricted)—a very low security label.[81] According to Stier, the director of Gedob's *Sonderzüge* group, one of his staff members was a Polish railroad official, Stanislaw Feix. The man was apparently allowed to see all the records. "Moreover," says Stier, "our files were in no way closed; they were lying around openly and could be seen by anyone having access to our offices."[82]

The very location of the death camps on heavily traveled trunk lines was a clue visible to railroad men and passengers alike. In the Warsaw directorate, the daily average of full trains was 124, and 40 to 48 of them traversed the section Warsaw–Malkinia/Treblinka.[83] There are photographs of Jewish deportees, including corpses, taken by a soldier from Austria at Siedlce. The troop train had halted there, and the Jews were being reloaded.[84] Another German soldier, traveling along Bełżec, left us a graphic description of his observations in a diary.[85]

Auschwitz was astride a main traffic artery. The freight yards of the Auschwitz railroad station contained forty-four parallel tracks; they were two miles long. Everyone, including the deportees who had to pass through, could see the customary big shield announcing the stop: Auschwitz. About one and one-half miles farther lay the entrance to the killing section of the camp, Birkenau. A railroad man (Hilse) who was transferred to the station observed that his post was located in the center of the camp ("mitten drin"); there were fences and guard towers on both sides of the tracks. The chimneys could be seen from moving trains; at night they were visible from a distance of twelve miles. "That meant," said another railroad functionary (Barthelmäss), "that the bodies were being burned publicly." He lived in the area and noticed that his windows were covered with a bluish film and that his apartment was filled with a sweetish odor. Trains emptied of their deportees were brought back to the station to be routed to a fumigation installation. Once, during a hot day, a loadmaster opened the car of such a train and was frightened to death: a blackened corpse fell out. The car was filled with the bodies of deportees who had died on the train, and camp personnel had forgotten to remove them.[86]

Regardless of rank, railroad men who were concerned with Jewish transports only had to harness their conscience and common sense to obtain an overview of the situation before them; and once they had taken that step, they could no longer bypass their reflections. So spoke a veteran of Reichsbahndirektion Oppeln who personally knew the layout of Auschwitz. He branded any contention to the contrary by one or another of his colleagues as "preposterous" (*töricht*).[87] The question, of course, is what kind of thoughts were generated by a procession of *Sonderzüge* with sealed-in victims moving to the east.

Let us first consider the literalist Friedrich vom Baur, Direktor of Ostbahn Bezirksdirektion Radom, whose territory covered Lublin. Asked about Jewish transports, he said in 1962:

> In this matter, I can point out that in 1942 a uniformed member of the SS looked me up in Lublin and asked me if it was possible to carry out Jewish transports to Bełżec by rail. When I asked what was to be done with the Jews over there, the SS man replied that Jews would be driven into the fields (*die*

Juden würden ins Gelände getrieben). The question concerning the possibility of carrying out Jewish transports I answered in the affirmative, because the possibility existed in fact (technically speaking) and besides, because I had not been informed that Jews were going to be killed in the Bełżec camp.

The timetables, at any rate, were written by the Gedob in Kraków; he had had nothing to do with them. Trains may have been assembled by his Direktion, but he would not have known such facts.[88]

A specialist in Gedob's section 33, Christian Leibhäuser, who does not exclude the possibility that his office participated in conferences affecting Jewish trains that crossed two or more Direktionen in the Generalgouvernement, says that already in 1942—and certainly thereafter—he had heard hints that Jews were being burned in camps, "that is, that they were killed there." Gassings were subjects of conversation as well. "In jargon, one also indicated that today there is going to be a new soap allocation; one wanted to say (ironically) that Jews were boiled into soap."[89]

Dr. Günther Lübbeke, who worked in Lublin, Lwów, and at the Gedob, had many indications of what was happening to the Jews. He had word about the Kiev massacre in the early fall of 1941 from an Organisation Todt official "in the open environment of a dining car." The Organisation Todt had been called on to blow up bodies when the SS could not cover them with earth. Later, after Stalingrad (in 1943), Lübbecke spent time with colleagues figuring out how many Jews had been brought into the Generalgouvernement with transports. The estimate was 600,000.[90]

Karl Becker, who headed the Kraków directorate in 1942 and who married a Polish woman, had a conversation with a Reichsbahnoberinspektor Raszik in which the latter declared "quite openly" that "our leading men were all criminals." Raszik did not give reasons for his conclusion, but Becker assumes that he had referred to the annihilation camps.[91]

Quite another tone was adopted by a Warsaw Reichsbahn official who told his successor about shootings of Jews. "I can still remember that he said in the conversation that children had run like sheep with the herd and the parents had done nothing to save them. German parents would naturally have defended their children."[92]

In the Transport Ministry itself there was also some reflection. Karl Heim, the director of section 212 who rifled through the *Sonderzüge* file, says that he discussed what he had seen there with an outside friend. The two came to the conclusion that, based on transport figures, Auschwitz must have been a metropolis.[93] A typist in E 2/21 tells of the agitation in the offices when a *Sonderzug* was unable to move between stations after the tracks had been hit by bombs. She believes it was a Jewish *Sonderzug*.[94]

Ganzenmüller's own secretary relates that the Staatssekretär himself had wondered about the camps, how people could be fed there and how they could be clothed. Once he returned from Hitler's headquarters, shaken, saying something to the effect that he did not really know why he was continuing. She assumes he referred to the continuation of the Jewish transports.[95]

The guards who repeatedly rode the trains were also capable of thought. One of them, a pious Baptist from Mannheim, began to pray aloud as soon as the train was in the vicinity of Auschwitz. A fellow guard (who observed him) asserts that he himself was an opponent of the regime, never a party member. "I was always a Socialist and my father belonged to the Socialist Party for fifty years. When we talked with each other—which was often—I always said that if there was still justice, things could not go on like that much longer."[96]

Stable Organization, Stable Careers

The Reichsbahn was a highly stable organization. One thinks of the typical Reichsbahn official as someone whose life was tied up with trains. Many railroad men worked at their jobs before 1933 and after 1945. Nazism did not interrupt their careers or change their personalities. Gerteis, a "convinced Christian," Schelp, a Quaker, Leibbrand, a railroad authority of international repute—who could have been more loyal, respectable, or dependable?

They were solid individuals, but not mindless robots. As intelligent men, they were capable of understanding the tenor of their time. They could not fail to obtain an "overview" of their situation; they could not "bypass" their reflections. The fact is that they were part of Nazi Germany, ruthless, relentless, and draconian practitioners in every respect.

Yet they survived its collapse, changing only their collective name from Reichsbahn to Bundesbahn. In the war crimes trials conducted by the Allied victors, leaders of I. G. Farben and other industrial enterprises were in the docket as defendants (because these firms were considered extensions of the German government), whereas the public railroad men were untouched as if they were employees in a private undertaking. A few, like Jacobi and Klemm, had been "carried off" by the Russians; some others, including Stange and Rau, were already old; but a substantial part of the cast in this story showed up again as members of West Germany's Bundesbahn. From the old Ostbahn alone, the new directories contained the names of vom Baur, Glas, Liebhäuser, Richter, Schweinoch, Stier—the list is a lengthy one. The Gedob's Albrecht Zahn, who signed orders scheduling death trains to Treblinka, became Bundesbahndirektor in charge of Stuttgart. Schelp of E 1 rose to the rank of Bundesbahnpräsident. Geitmann, who had run the Oppeln Direktion (which included Auschwitz), moved up to be one of the four members of the Bundesbahn's top directorate—one of the crassest promotions in postwar German history.

The books and memoirs written by railroad men speak of the Second World War as an epitomization of achievement. Werner Pischel, an Ost-bahn veteran, and also Kreidler refer to the railroad preparations for the onslaught on the USSR as the greatest mobilization of railway transport in the world. In the Nuremberg Verkehrsarchiv, a map of the Reichsbahn was reconstituted to show its network in November 1942—the time of its greatest extent. Upstairs, above the archive in the museum, there is a bust of Reichsminister Dorpmüller, who headed the Reichsbahn before and during the war.

Except for Pischel, no one speaks publicly of the Jewish trains. Pischel wrote about them carefully from secondary sources only.[97] Today, the Reichsbahn's participation in the destruction process is a more carefully guarded secret than it was at the time of the *Sonderzüge*. And if present-day Germany, taken as a whole, quietly concurs in this burial, there is good reason for the silence. A generation after the end of the Nazi regime, the issue is not which old man should go to prison or which should lose his pension. It is not even the reputation of this or that former Reichsbahnoberinspek-tor. It is the more basic problem of what Nazi Germany really was and what its history may still mean.

In a word, the role of the German railroads in the destruction of the Jews opens profound questions about the substance and ramifications of the entire Nazi Reich. Through the years, the railroads have not been con-sidered a significant component of a political structure; yet they were an indispensable part of the destructive machine. They were not assumed to have beliefs, but they were capable of making drastic decisions. At the same time, the Reichsbahn was as much a self-contained structure, cor-porate in form, and as insulated from pressure by the very nature of its technical functions, as any organization could possibly be. The railroads were also a true system in the modern sense of the term—the very nature of train movements from one end of Europe to the other necessitated a perpetual effort to maintain the circulatory flow.

The deep involvement of the railroads in the destruction process is thus a fact that may no longer be discarded as ancillary or inconsequential. It illuminates and defines the very concept of "totalitarianism." The Jews could not be destroyed by one Führer or one order. That unprecedented event was a product of multiple initiatives, as well as lengthy negotiations and repeated adjustments among separate power structures, which differed from one another in their traditions and customs but which were united in their unfathomable will to push the Nazi regime to the limits of its de-structive potential.

Notes

1. For a broad discussion of the subject, see Robert Wolfe, ed., *Captured German and Related Records—A National Archives Conference* (Athens: Ohio University Press, 1974).

2. Transport Ministry (signed Hesse) to Prosecutor's Office in Dortmund, 16 February 1966, Landgericht Düsseldorf, Case Ganzenmüller, vol. 6.

3. A few background materials, preserved by railroaders, are referred to and included in unpublished studies now located at the Nuremberg Verkehrsarchiv. A relatively important hoard was kept as late as April 1976 by a former Ministerialrat (once chief liaison officer of the Reichsbahn with the army), Eugen Kreidler. See his book, *Die Eisenbahnen im Machtbereich der Achsenmächte während des Zweiten Weltkrieges* (Göttingen: Musterschmidt-Verlag, 1975). The sources in his possession are listed on p. 400. Kreidler's account is the most exhaustive history of the wartime Reichsbahn, but not once does he mention Jews.

4. Access was denied to me. German Democratic Republic/Interior Ministry/State Archives Administration to the author, 19 February 1976.

5. Much of this paper is built on the work of German and Austrian prosecutors. My particular thanks go to Dr. Adalbert Rückerl, director of the Zentrale Stelle der Landesjustizverwaltungen in Ludwigsburg, for his exceptional hospitality; to Dr. Peter Hofmann, prosecutor at the Vienna Landesgericht, for his personal notes; to Dr. Kunze of the Railway Document Center at Frankfurt and Mr. Illenseer at the German Verkehrsarchiv in Nuremberg for their patient explanations of technical railroad material; and to Dr. Böhmer and Judge Monschau of the Düsseldorf Landgericht for their administrative assistance. Most valuable was my early use of the indictment of Ganzenmüller, whose principal author is Dr. Alfred Spiess, presently the chief prosecutor in Wuppertal. My university granted me sabbatical leave for the spring of 1976 to pursue this research.

6. Dokumentationsdienst der DB, *Dokumentarische Enzyklopädie V—Eisenbahn und Eisenbahner zwischen 1941 und 1945* (Frankfurt am Main: Redactor Verlag, 1973), 110.

7. On Ganzenmüller's appointment and career, see Albert Speer, *Inside the Third Reich* (New York: Macmillan, 1970), 222–25; Kreidler, *Eisenbahnen*, 205–6; Prosecution at Düsseldorf to Landgericht Düsseldorf, 16 March 1970, transmitting indictment of Ganzenmüller, File No. 8 Js 430/67, in Zentrale Stelle at Ludwigsburg and in Landgericht Düsseldorf; Statement and answers to questions by Ganzenmüller, 7 October 1964, Case Ganzenmüller, 5:216–17.

8. See the annual *Verzeichnis der oberen Reichsbahnbeamten*, particularly for 1941 and 1943.

9. Kreidler, *Eisenbahnen*. See also the detailed description, written with considerable legal finesse, by Ministerialrat Dr. Werner Haustein, "Das Werden der Grossdeutschen Reichsbahn im Rahmen des Grossdeutschen Reiches," *Die Reichsbahn* 18 (1942): 76–88, 114–25.

10. Interrogation of Willy Hilse, undated (circa 1964) in Frankfurt am Main, Landesgericht Vienna, Case Novak, File 1416/16, vol. 12, 605–7.

11. Deutsches Kursbuch, *Jahresfahrplan*, 1942/43, effective 4 May 1942.

12. Eichmann to Reichsbahn, 20 February 1941, Case Ganzenmüller, special 4:4:105.

13. Treibe to Reichsbahndirektionen, copies to Gedob, Protectorate railways, and Mitteleuropäisches Reisebüro, 26 July 1941, Case Ganzenmüller, special 4:3:47–55.

14. Reichsbahndirektion Oppeln to Ministry, 28 February 1942, and E 1/15 to Oppeln, March (?) 1942, Case Ganzenmüller, special 4:4:117–18.

15. Reichsbahndirektion Vienna (signed by Dr. Bockhorn) to Slovak Transport Ministry, copies in house and to Dresden, Oppeln, and Mitteleuropäisches Reisebüro, 27 April 1942, Yad Vashem archives (Jerusalem), M-5/18(1).

16. Slovak Transport Ministry to Gedob and Reichsbahndirektion Vienna, 12 August 1942, Yad Vashem M-5/18(1); Vienna (Dr. Zacke) to Slovak Transport Ministry, 23 September 1942, Yad Vashem M-5/18(1).

17. E 1/16 to Reichsbahndirektionen Karlsruhe, Cologne, Münster, Saarbrücken, copies to Hauptverkehrsdirektionen Brussels and Paris, Plenipotentiary in Utrecht, and Amtsrat Stange, 14 July 1942, Case Ganzenmüller, special 4:3:56.

18. Remarks by Eichmann at Düsseldorf conference, 14 March 1942. Case Novak, 17:203–7. Novak (in Eichmann's office) to Höss (Auschwitz commander), 23 January 1942, Case Novak, 17:295. Testimony by Novak, 4 December 1969, trial transcript, Case Novak, 15:304–5.

19. See Reichsbahn Traffic Office in Łódź to Gestapo in Łódź, 5 May 1942, Zentrale Stelle in Ludwigsburg, vol. Polen 315, 445.

20. See the Minsk folder in Institut für Zeitgeschichte, Munich, Fb 85/2, passim.

21. Order by Dr. Jacobi (Generalbetriebsleitung Ost/PW), 8 August 1942, Institut für Zeitgeschichte, Fb85/2, 217–19. For Jacobi's position, see Figure 2.3. Lodz Electrical Suburban Lines to Gestapo Łódź, 19 May 1942, Zentrale Stelle Ludwigsburg, vol. Polen 315, 388.

22. Reichsvereinigung directive of 3 December 1941, Israel Police Document 738. Maedel to Mayer and Kallenbach (all in Finance Ministry), 14 December 1942, Bundesarchiv Koblenz, R 2/12222.

23. Gettoverwaltung financial statements, 31 March and 30 April 1942, listing transport costs aggregating 112,143 Reichsmarks. Zentrale Stelle Ludwigsburg, vol. Polen 315, 73, 75.

24. Dr. Siegert (Himmler's office) to Finance Ministry, 17 August 1942, and subsequent correspondence, Bundesarchiv Koblenz, R 2/12158. The military commander was confiscating Jewish property in France.

25. Nederlandsche Spoorwegen to Zentralstelle für jüdische Auswanderung, 15 May and 10 June 1944, and Reichsbahn Plenipotentiary (signed Dr. Fritzen) to Security Police Commander in Holland, 10 August 1944, German records microfilmed at Alexandria, VA, T175/Roll 485.

26. Rau to High Command of the Army, 1 March 1944, and subsequent correspondence in Bundesarchiv Koblenz, R 2/14133.

27. Statement by Dr. Gustav Dilli, 15 August 1967, Case Ganzenmüller, 18:31, insert, 18–26.

28. Statement by Novak, Case Novak, 8:71.

29. Statement by Gerda Boyce, 2 April 1969, Case Ganzenmüller, 18:86–92.

30. Statement by Karl Heim, 18 April 1969, Case Ganzenmüller, 18:98–103.

31. Kreidler, *Eisenbahnen*, 278–89.

32. Statement by Dr. Fritz Schelp in letter to prosecutor Dr. Uchmann, 14 July 1967, Case Ganzenmüller, 18:31, insert 3–7.

33. Statement by Schelp, 16 February 1966, Case Ganzenmüller, 6:139–42.

34. According to Walter Rohde, E 2/22 (later E 2/23) requests containing estimated requirements for rolling stock were sent from 21 to E 1/10 (freight cars) for initial approval. His statement of 7 July 1967, Case Ganzenmüller, 18:31, insert 3–7.

35. Directives by Leibbrand, 30 April 1940 and 14 July 1941, Case Ganzenmüller, special 4:4:109–111, red numbered. Both directives were marked "21." Their language was so involuted that it might have been disregarded for such short-haul programs at Katowice–Auschwitz or Łódź–Kulmhof.

36. Kreidler, *Eisenbahnen*, 204.

37. Text in Case Ganzenmüller, special 4:3:37.

38. Statement by Walther Stier, 9 September 1969, Case Novak, 6:405.

39. German Foreign Office (signed Krieger) to legation in Bratislava, 7 June 1942, Case Novak, 17:294.

40. The Generaldirektion der Ostbahn was represented by Stier in most conferences involving transports to the Generalgouvernement. Stier attended the second Bratislava meeting. Summary of German-Slovak railway conference held on 10 November 1942, Yad Vashem, M-5/18 (2).

41. Wehrmachtverkehrsdirektion Paris/33 (signed Möhl) on Auschwitz trains to P and PW among others, Case Ganzenmüller, special 4:4:12. Railways to Prague (signed Staudinger) on Theresienstadt-Minsk transport to P and PW among others. 5 September 1942, Inst. f. Zeitgeschichte, Fb 85/2, 209. The signature of Staudinger had designation BBV (for Bahnbevollmächtigte)—field official with authority to handle military trains. The BBV in Prague is one of [the] recipients of telegram on Vienna-Minsk train by Schober (Reichsbahndirektion Vienna/33 B) 27 May 1942, Fb 85/2, 282.

42. Excerpt of timetable for Düsseldorf-Trawniki train (undated), Zentrale Stelle Ludwigsburg, folder IDS 243, 26, and timetable for Aachen-Theresienstadt train scheduled for 25–26 July 1942, Zentrale Stelle Ludwigsburg, folder IDS 243, 290.

43. A "protocol" signed by Klemm is included in the indictment of Ganzenmüller. It is the record of a conference held 26 and 28 September 1942, on transports from the War- saw, Radom, Kraków, Lublin, and Lwów districts to Treblinka, Bełżec, and Sobibór. Also mentioned are Romanian transports that subsequently did not materialize. The text is a somewhat garbled retranslation into German. It appears to be derived from a translation found in Romania.

44. Interrogation of Stier, 16 March 1963, Case Novak, 16:355–57. Also, his statement of 9 September 1969, Case Novak, 16:405, and the testimony in the Novak trial, 10 April 1972, 18:344–53.

45. Statements by Gerhard Reelitz, 26 April 1967, and Otto Purschke, 28 April 1967. Case Ganzenmüller, 14:84–90, 96–97.

46. Wolkowysk in the Białystok district was a reloading point. See, for example, Fahr- plananordnung (timetable order) of Reichsbahndirektion Königsberg/33 (signed Exner), 7 May 1942, on several Vienna-Minsk trains. Inst. f. Zeitgeschichte, Fb 85/2, 264–65.

47. See explanation in statement by Robert Bringmann, 29 June 1967, Case Ganzen- müller, 16:161, insert 11–14. For use of a Bedarfsfahrplan in France, see Hauptverkehrsdi- rektion Paris/33 (signed Weckmann) to Security Police in Paris, 30 April 1943, Yad Vashem, O-9/23. Gedob/33 in Fahrplananordnung of 25 August 1942 (signed Zahn) specifically mentions that Bedarfsfahrplan might be preempted by armed forces. Zentral Stelle Lud- wigsburg, folder Polen 162, film 6, 181.

48. Gedob 30H, Fahrplananordnung of 26 March 1943 (signed Schmid), Zentral Stelle Ludwigsburg, folder Polen 162, film 6, 192–93. For trains to Treblinka in Sonderplan, see telegram by Schmid, Zentral Stelle Ludwigsburg, folder Polen 162, film 6, 200. H = Hilfsar- beiter, a backup specialist covering for incumbent.

49. Summary of discussion between Transport Minister Dorpmüller and General Gercke, 10 November 1940, Alexandria document H 12/101.2. The item was not microfilmed. Order by Daluege (Chief of Order Police), 24 October 1941, Nuremberg trials document PS-3921.

50. Nuremberg Verkehrsarchiv, folder mm, contains partial reconstructed figures on Reichsbahndirektion Oppeln projects at Auschwitz among other localities.

51. As early as January 1940, Ganzenmüller's predecessor, Staatssekretär Kleinmann, noted a lack of personnel for a number of special projects including "the prospective reset- tlement of Jews." Kleinmann to Ley (German Labor Front) with copy to Gercke, 8 January 1940, H 12/101.2. By 1942, trained German personnel were stretched thin through occu- pied Europe.

The car problem reached a critical stage in the spring and summer of 1942, at the height of the offensive deep in Russia. See Kreidler, *Eisenbahnen*, 228; statement by Ganzenmüller,

7 October 1964, Case Ganzenmüller, 5:216–17. Car scarcity became acute again at the end of 1943 and in 1944.

Traffic bottlenecks occurred periodically, but became frequent and serious under Allied bombing from 1943. See Kreidler, *Eisenbahnen*, passim.

52. Kreidler, *Eisenbahnen*, 230.

53. Summary of IV B 4 conference dated 6 March 1942, Case Novak, 17:203–7.

54. Kreidler, *Eisenbahnen*, 247–48.

55. Jacobi order, 16 January 1943, Inst. f. Zeitgeschichte, Fb 85/2, 203–5.

56. See excerpts of report by Police Captain Salitter, commander of guards on class 2 priority train, 26 December 1941, in H. G. Adler, *Der verwaltete Mensch* (Tübingen: J.C.B. Mohr, 1974), 461–65.

57. Statement by Anton Kaes (Warsaw directorate), 1 October 1968, Case Ganzenmüller, 17:66–69.

58. Ibid.

59. Salitter report in Adler, *Der verwaltete Mensch*, 464.

60. Reichsbahndirektion Vienna/33 H (signed Eigl) to section 18, 5 May 1941 and 12 March 1942, Zentrale Stelle Ludwigsburg, folder Verschiedenes 301, AAe 112, at 232 and 249.

61. Diary of Generalgouverneur Frank, 18 June 1942, Nuremberg trials document PS-2233.

62. Ganzenmüller to Wolff, 28 July 1942, Nuremberg trials document NO-2207, and his statement of 7 October 1964, Case Ganzenmüller, 5:216–27.

63. Statement by Erich Richter, 11 June 1969, Case Ganzenmüller, 19:5–12. Gedob Fahrplananordnungen (signed Richter), 22 August, 15 September, and 22 September 1942, Zentrale Stelle Ludwigsburg, vol. Polen 162, film 6, 179–80, 184–89.

64. Krüger to Himmler, 5 December 1942, Himmler files, folder No. 94, Library of Congress.

65. Order by Jacobi, 16 January 1943, Inst. f. Zeitgeschichte, Fb 85/2, 203–8.

66. Kreidler, *Eisenbahnen*, 246.

67. At the Düsseldorf conference, Eichmann said that cars for Jewish deportations had been made available with the "agreement" of the Armed Forces High Command, Novak case, 17:203–7. Faced with a shutdown in December 1942, Krüger urged Himmler to approach the armed forces. See his letter of 5 December 1942, Himmler Files, folder No. 94, Library of Congress. Klemm mentioned the Wehrmachttransportleitung Südost in connection with the planned Romanian transports. See the text (somewhat unclear in retranslation) of conference, 26 and 28 September 1942, in Ganzenmüller indictment, 149–51. [A translation appears in this book as Document A.2.] Ganzenmüller asserts that SS clearance with transport officers, at least locally, was essential. His statement of 7 October 1964, Case Ganzenmüller, 5:216–27. However, only an early example of such practice is on record. Memorandum by Dannecker (an Eichmann representative), 11 October 1939, and Günther to Braune (Security Service), 23 October 1939, Zentrale Stelle Ludwigsburg, folder CSSR, Red No. 148, 79–82, 49–54.

68. No record of this conference has been found. Some of the details were described in testimony by Novak in several of his trials, 16–18 November 1964, 13:39–41, 26 and 28 September 1966, 14:293, 303–24, 20 and 21 March 1972, 18:96, 155–60. Also, statement by Dr. Laszlo Lulay, 18 February 1948 and his interrogation of 7 July 1960, Case Novak, vol. 15, folder at 425a. Lulay, Hungarian police interpreter, attended the meeting.

69. Report by Lt. Col. Ferenczy (Hungarian gendarmerie), 9 July 1944, Case Novak, 12:427.

70. Testimony by Novak, 16 and 18 November 1964, Case Novak, 13:39–41.

71. Plenipotentiary of German Transport Ministry with Slovak Transport Ministry to Slovak Ministry, 1 March 1945, facsimile in Livia Rothkirchen, *The Destruction of Slovak Jewry* (Jerusalem: Yad Vashem, 1961), facing 224.

72. SS and Police Leader Globocnik (Lublin district) to Himmler, undated, probably autumn 1942, Nuremberg trials, document PS-4042.

73. Report by Kammler (Construction Office of SS-Economic-Administrative Main Office), 19 April 1944, in Jüdisches Historisches Institut Warschau, *Faschismus-Getto-Massenmord* (Berlin: Rütten & Loening, 1961), 424–26.

74. Undated final report of Einsatzstab Rosenberg, Dienststelle Westen, Nuremberg trials document L-188. For direct negotiations between Einsatzstab and Reichsbahn, see Dienststelle Westen, report of 16 June 1944, Alexandria, T175/Roll 225.

75. See statistical reports of Judenrat Warsaw/Labor Division, 26 May and 16 June 1942, listing 567 and 786 ghetto Jews respectively, working for Reichsbahn offices in Warsaw. Zentrale Stelle Ludwigsburg, folder Polen 365a, 735, 736.

76. Final report of Einsatzstab Rosenberg, L-188.

77. One could effect being transferred by means of "stealth." Statement by Robert Bringmann (Gedob), 29 June 1967, Case Ganzenmüller, 16:161, insert at 11–14.

78. Inst. f. Zeitgeschichte, Fb 85/2.

79. Zentrale Stelle Ludwigsburg, folder IDS 243, 290.

80. Fahrplananordnung of Haupteisenbahndirektion Mitte/33, 13 May 1942, Inst. f. Zeitgeschichte, Fb 85/2, 270–71.

81. See his statement of 11 June 1969, Case Ganzenmüller, 19:5–12. Richter was Hilfs-arbeiter for 33 and 34.

82. Interrogation of Stier, 16 March 1963, Case Novak, 16:355–57.

83. Statement by Kurt Becker, 8 April 1965, Case Ganzenmüller, 6:87–93. Becker served in Warsaw from November 1939 to February 1942 and from August 1943.

84. Gitta Sereny, *Into that Darkness* (New York: McGraw Hill, 1974), 158–59, and photographs after page 192.

85. Notes by a non-commissioned officer (Wilhelm Cornides), 21 August 1942, Inst. f. Zeitgeschichte, ED 81.

86. Testimony by Adolf Johann Barthelmäss in Novak trial, 2 December 1964, 13:281–89, and his statement of 11 April 1967, Case Novak, 16:338. The witness lived in Auschwitz. Also, interrogation of Willy Hilse, ca. 1964, Case Novak, 12:605, and his testimony in the Novak trial, 13:248–57. Hilse worked in the Auschwitz freight yard. Both men described incidents with bodies.

87. Statement by Ulrich Brand, 23 June 1967, Case Ganzenmüller, 16:161, folder at 7–10.

88. Statement by Friedrich vom Baur, 11 May 1962, Case Ganzenmüller, vol. 5, red number 36–38.

89. Statement by Christian Leibhäuser, 28 August 1961, Case Ganzenmüller, 5:154–59.

90. Statement by Dr. Günther Lübbeke, 5 December 1968, Case Ganzenmüller, 18:22–28. Lübbeke later became Bundesbahndirektor and permanent member of the staff of the World Bank in Washington, DC.

91. Statement by Karl Becker, 15 October 1968, Case Ganzenmüller, 18:119–24.

92. Statement by Dr. Paul Schröter, 1 March 1968, Case Ganzenmüller, 16:56–63. His predecessor was Dr. Lange.

93. Statement by Heim, 18 April 1969, Case Ganzenmüller 18:98–103. Compare statement by Dr. Franz Verbeck, Gedob/9 (Passenger Traffic), 5 October 1960, Case Ganzenmüller, 5:129–31. Verbeck observed that all the *Sonderzüge* "no matter where they came from went to some small locality in eastern Poland."

94. Statement by Gerda Boyce, 2 April 1969, Case Ganzenmüller, 18:86–92.

95. Statement by Ursel McKee, 3 December 1968, Case Ganzenmüller, 18:8–16.

96. Testimony by Ernst Göx (police) in Novak trial, 6 April 1972, 18:330–32.

97. Werner Pischel, "Die Generaldirektion der Ostbahn in Krakau 1939–1945," *Archiv für Eisenbahnwesen* 74 (1964): 46.

Bibliography

Adler, H. G. *Der verwaltete Mensch.* Tübingen: J.C.B. Mohr, 1974.

Dokumentationsdienst der DB. *Dokumentarische Enzyklopädie V—Eisenbahn und Eisenbahner zwischen 1941 und 1945.* Frankfurt am Main: Redactor Verlag, 1973.

Haustein, Werner. "Das Werden der Grossdeutschen Reichsbahn im Rahmen des Grossdeutschen Reiches." *Die Reichsbahn* 18 (1942): 76–125.

Jüdisches Historisches Institut Warschau, *Faschismus-Getto-Massenmord.* Berlin: Rütten & Loening, 1960.

Kreidler, Eugen. *Die Eisenbahnen im Machtbereich der Achsenmächte während des Zweiten Weltkrieges.* Göttingen: Musterschmidt-Verlag, 1975.

Pischel, Werner. "Die Generaldirektion der Ostbahn in Krakau 1939–1945." *Archiv für Eisenbahnwesen* 74 (1964): 1–80.

Rothkirchen, Livia. *The Destruction of Slovak Jewry.* Jerusalem: Yad Vashem, 1961.

Sereny, Gitta. *Into that Darkness.* New York: McGraw Hill, 1974.

Speer, Albert. *Inside the Third Reich.* New York: Macmillan, 1970.

Wolfe, Robert, ed. *Captured German and Related Records—A National Archives Conference.* Athens: Ohio University Press, 1974.

DOCUMENT SECTION

A. Conferences
   1. Berlin, RSHA IV B 4 conference, 6 March 1942
   2. Protocol by Bruno Klemm of the conference held in Berlin, 26
      and 28 September 1942, concerning the evacuation of Jews of the
      General Government and the dispatching of Romanian Jews into
      the General Government

B. Correspondence about Obtaining Trains
   1. Note by Theodor Dannecker, 13 May 1942
   2. Note by Kurt Lischka to RSHA IV B 4, 15 May 1942
   3. Note by Dannecker to RSHA IV B 4, 16 June 1942
   4. Note by Dannecker, 18 June 1942
   5. Correspondence between Albert Ganzenmüller and Karl Wolff,
      28 July–13 August 1942
   6. Note by Heinrich Himmler to Ganzenmüller, 20 January 1943

C. Transport Schedules
   1. Railroad Direction Office Königsberg, Timetable Nr. 12, 7 May 1942
   2. Main Railroad Direction Office Mitte, Minsk, Timetable Nr. 40,
      13 May 1942
   3. Karl Jacobi of Gedob to National Railroad Direction Offices and
      others, 16 January 1943

D. Preparing Deportations
   1. Report by Police Assistant Hermann Waldbillig concerning provi-
      sion of train equipment to transport Jews to and from Düsseldorf,
      17 April 1942

2. Guidelines for activated officials. Appendix to the urgent letter of the Secret Police, State Police Office Frankfurt am Main, 21 August 1942

E. Transport Reports
1. Confidential Report on the Evacuation of Jews to Riga on 11–17 December 1941 by Police Captain Salitter, 26 December 1941
2. Report of Police Reserve Lieutenant Fischmann on escorting a transport of Jews from Vienna to Sobibór on 14–20 June 1942, 20 June 1942
3. Report of Police Lieutenant Westermann on two transports of Jews from Kolomea [Kołomyja] to Bełżec on 7–10 September 1942, 14 September 1942

F. Survivor Accounts
1. Postwar account by Hilde Sherman-Zander, Jewish survivor, of the transport from Düsseldorf to Riga, 10–14 December 1941, the same transport as described in the Salitter report
2. Postwar account by Rudolf Reder, Jewish survivor, of his transport from Lviv (Lemberg) to Bełżec, 10–11 August 1942

Document A.1. Berlin, RSHA IV B 4 conference, 6 March 1942 [Israel State Archives, Israel Police Bureau 6, Eichmann Document 119]

Düsseldorf, 9 March 1942

Report on the meeting that took place in the Reich Security Main Office IV B 4 on 6 March 1942.

SS-Obersturmbannführer Eichmann began by speaking first of all about the further evacuation of 55,000 Jews from the Altreich [pre-1938 Germany] as well as the Ostmark [Austria] and the Protectorate [Bohemia and Moravia].

Among others in this connection, Prague with 20,000 and Vienna with 18,000 Jews to be evacuated will have the greatest share. The size of the other transports will be determined in proportion to the number of Jews still present in the district of each Gestapo head office. In this connection Düsseldorf is again allotted a transport of 1,000 Jews.

In this regard SS-Obersturmbannführer Eichmann pointed out that the existing guidelines, above all regarding age, infirmity, etc., must be most strictly observed, because with the transport to Riga the Jewish council in Riga protested through the Gauleiters Lohse and Meyer to SS-Obergruppenführer Heydrich that some 40–45 cases were wrongly evacuated. Although the majority of these cases after detailed examination proved to be totally justified evacuations, the avoidance of such complaints must under all circumstances be strived for. Thus SS-Obergruppenführer Heydrich makes the Gestapo office heads personally responsible in this regard for the implementation of the guidelines.

So that individual Gestapo offices "are not further subject to the temptation to get rid of their undesirable old Jews," SS-Obersturmbannführer Eichmann provided reassurance that in the course of this summer or fall these Jews remaining in the Old Reich will most likely be deported to Theresienstadt, which is earmarked as an "Old People's Ghetto." This city is now being cleared, and temporarily some 15–20,000 Jews from the Protectorate can be moved there. This is being done in order "to preserve our external image."

The Gau- and Kreisleiters must be informed before the evacuations, as many Gauleiters had complained that they had received no information concerning such drastic measures.

SS-Obersturmbannführer Eichmann then gave the floor to individual experts; next came a presentation on the matter of property rights.

The seizure of property has been considerably simplified through the 11th Ordinance [to the Reich Citizenship Law]. The forms for property registration have been changed accordingly and are going out to the individual Gestapo district offices immediately. The old forms are no longer to be used. The forms are to be filled out with greatest exactitude because the Jews have attempted many "tricks." The number of Jews to be evacuated, as well as their residences, are to be given to the Finance Offices.

Under no circumstances may the Jews learn of the preparations for evacuation. Thus absolute secrecy is necessary.

The so-called "Special Account W" [Sonderkonto W] is available to Referat IV B 4 of the Reich Security Main Office, because in accordance with the 11th Ordinance the RSHA no longer has access to Jewish property. In order to provide this account with sufficient money, it is requested to encourage the Jews in the near future to make considerable "contributions" to Account W. Apparently because of the misunderstanding that the Jews directly benefit from the account, little of value has been deposited up to now.

In agreement with the foreign exchange office, the sum of 50 RM to be taken by each Jew must be provided.

The next presentation dealt with the technical implementation of the transport. It is important that for the moment the timing of the transports cannot be precisely scheduled. In the Old Reich, only empty Russian trains/worker transports that would go back empty to the General Government are available, and now in agreement with the OKR [Reichsbahn leadership] will be used by the RSHA.

The departure date will be made known to the Gestapo district offices six days in advance by telephone for the sake of quick transmission and maintenance of secrecy under the code word DA. The call is to be confirmed immediately by telegraph to Referat IV B 4.

The departure hours are to be learned from the travel schedule that must be strictly adhered to.

The trains accommodate only 700 people, but 1,000 Jews must be loaded in them. It is recommended that a sufficient number of freight cars for the baggage are punctually ordered from the Reichsbahn. Likewise a passenger car for the escort commando. If need be, however, one must put up with a car of the Russian train.

The leader of the escort commando must be instructed to insure that upon arrival at the destination, the baggage cars from the Altreich return immediately.

An exchange of experiences followed between the Gestapo offices that had already carried out evacuations and the others that faced this task for the first time.

The meeting ended around 16:30.

(signature)
Polizei-Inspektor

Document A.2. Protocol by Bruno Klemm of the conference held in Berlin on 26 and 28 September 1942, concerning the evacuation of Jews of the General Government and the dispatching of Romanian Jews into the General Government

Note: The original German document has not been found. A wartime Romanian translation survived in the Romanian archives [published in Jean Ancel, ed., *Documents Concerning the Fate of Romanian Jewry during the Holocaust*, vol. 10 (New York: Beate Klarsfeld Foundation, 1986), 237–38]. The United Restitution Organization published a re-translation (*Rückübersetzung*) into German in *Dokumente über Methoden der Judenverfolgung im Ausland* (Frankfurt am Main, 1959), 75–76. This volume presents an English translation, based on the Romanian translation and the German re-translation—despite the potentially corrupting effects on the text of so many linguistic transitions—precisely because it provides extraordinarily rare insight into a planning conference for Jewish transports both within the General Government and from abroad. That said, the proposals of Reinhard Heydrich presented to this planning conference were not completely fulfilled. No deportation trains ever delivered Romanian Jews to the General Government. Neither did Heydrich receive the maximum number of trains that he requested from the Ostbahn. Nonetheless, some 380,000 Polish Jews from the General Government and the adjoining district of Białystok were sent to the death camps of Operation Reinhard from the beginning of October to mid-December 1942.

Agenda:
1. The evacuation of 600,000 Jews of the General Government.
2. The dispatching of 280,000 Romanian Jews into the General Government.

EVACUATION OF POLISH JEWS

To point 1) Urgent transports, proposed by the Chief of Security Police and SD [Security Service], namely:

2 trains per day from the district of Warsaw to Treblinka
1 train per day from the district of Radom to Treblinka
1 train per day from the district of Kraków to Bełżec and
1 train per day from the district of Lemberg to Bełżec

must be carried out with 200 freight cars, that have already been made available for this purpose by the General Directorate of the Eastern Railroad in Kraków [Generaldirektion der Ostbahn in Krakau], insofar as this is feasible.

After the completion of the restoration of the Lublin–Chełm line, probably on or after 1 November 1942, the other urgent transports can also be carried out, namely:

1 train per day from the district of Radom to Sobibór
1 train per day from the northern region of the district of Lublin to Bełżec and
1 train per day from the central region of the district of Lublin to Sobibór

insofar as this is feasible and the required number of freight cars is available.

It must be assumed that after the reduction of potato transports the Main Car Allocation Office [Hauptwagenamt] will have the possibility to assign to the General Directorate of the Eastern Railroad in Kraków the additional cars that are necessary for these trains, so that the desired train traffic proposed here can be completed by the end of the year.

DEPORTATION OF ROMANIAN JEWS

To point 2) the Romanian railway [representatives] telegraphed on the day of the conference that they could not attend the conference for technical reasons and asked for the conference to be postponed.

The conference that took place without the representatives of the Romanian railway produced the following results.

The departure station in Romania for the special trains is Adjud on the Ploesti-Cernautzi line, the border station with the General Government is Sniatyn [Śniatyn], the destination is Bełżec.

It is envisaged that a special train, composed of 50 freight cars and one passenger car (for the escort personnel) for the transport of 2,000 people, shall run every second day. In order to avoid that it returns empty, German covered freight cars that are already in Romania or will arrive there will be used.

The general representative of the German railway in Bucharest, together with the Romanian railway, will be requested to arrange that the cars for carrying out the transports will be made available, though probably somewhat later than originally intended, in agreement with T.K. Bucharest [Transportkommando Bucharest?] and WTL Süd Ost [Wehrmachttransportleitung or Military Transport Directorate South East?].

The handover of the special trains by the C. F. R. [Romanian national railway] will be carried out punctually on the transportation days, in agreement with the General Directorate of the Ostbahn in Kraków, so that they can depart from Sniatyn in the direction of Lemberg at 1:03.

Klemm

Document B.1. Note by Theodor Dannecker, Head of the Jewish Office under the Commander of the Security Police and the Security Service (SD) for Belgium and France, 13 May 1942 [Memorial de la Shoah, Paris, Centre du documentation Juive contemporaine, XXVb-29]

IV J SA 225 a   Paris, 13 May 1942
DAN/Bir

    Re: Setting aside rolling stock for Jewish transports

1. Note:

Major Weber, the liaison officer of the Railroad Transportation Office with the Air Force, appeared here a little while ago. The conversation turned to reserving rolling stock for the deportation of Jews. According to Major Weber, Lieutenant General Kohl, the chief of the Railroad Transportation Office, takes a strong personal interest in the Jewish problem. I therefore declared myself ready to brief him on Jewish questions in France, if the general so wished.

General Kohl then let me know by telephone that he would welcome it if both of us would confer with him on 13 May 1942 at 11 a.m.

In the conversation that lasted an hour and a quarter, I gave the general an overview of Jewish questions and policy in France. I could establish that he is an uncompromising opponent of the Jews and that he agreed 100 percent with a final solution of the Jewish question that seeks the complete annihilation of the enemy. He also revealed himself as an enemy of the political churches.

At the end, Lieutenant General Kohl said the following to me in Major Weber's presence:

"I am delighted that we have met and thus established a connection with each other. You may discuss future transports with my responsible assistant. If you tell me, I want to ship off 10,000 or 20,000 Jews from France to the east, you may expect in every case that I will place the necessary rolling stock and locomotives at your service."

The general explained further that he regards the prompt solution of the Jewish question in occupied France as a vital necessity for the occupation troops, for which reason he takes a radical stance and supports its execution, even at the risk of being seen as brutal by certain people.

2. Submitted to SS-Standartenführer Dr. Knochen for his information.

3. Submitted to SS-Obersturmführer Lischka for his information.

4. Return to IV J.

Signed Dannecker, SS-Hauptsturmführer

Document B.2. Note by Kurt Lischka, Commander of the Security Police and the Security Service (SD), to RSHA IV B 4, Paris, 15 May 1942 [Memorial de la Shoah, Paris, Centre du documentation Juive contemporaine, XXVb-29]

Teletype

IV J—SA 225 a   Paris, 15 May 1942
Dan/Ge.

URGENT! PRESENT IMMEDIATELY!

To the Reich Security Main Office
— IV B 4 —
BERLIN

   Re: Setting aside rolling stock for Jewish transports
   File Reference: none

Establishing a good connection with Lieutenant General Kohl, the chief of the Railroad Transport Section (ETRA), has succeeded. Lieutenant General Kohl, who is an absolute opponent of Jews, has promised to provide all necessary railroad material and locomotives for the deportation of Jews. Accordingly, at least 10 trains can in the near future roll out of France.

I request notification, with reference to the various conversations of SS-Hauptsturmführer Dannecker with your office, whether and in what timeframe a larger number of Jews can be taken away and what camp is appropriate to receive them.

Because further roundups of Jews are necessary, but only a limited number of camps are available, I would be grateful initially for immediate removal of 5,000 Jews.

Signed Lischka, Sturmbannführer

Drafted by Dannecker

Document B.3. Note by Dannecker to RSHA IV B 4, 16 June 1942 [Nuremberg Document RF 1218]

IV J—SA 24   Paris, 16 June 1942
Dan/S.

Teletype Message
Urgent! Present immediately!
Secret!

To the Reich Security Main Office
IV B 4
Berlin

    Re: Jewish transports from France
    File Reference: Assignment from SS-Obersturmbannf. Eichmann to
    SS-Hauptstuf. Dannecker of 11 June 1942

The Railroad Transport Section (Etra, Paris) is for the following reasons unable to keep the promise that Lieutenant General Kohl made earlier to reserve rolling stock:

1.) In recent weeks in preparation for the operations in the east 37,000 cargo cars, 800 passenger cars, and 1,000 locomotives have been removed suddenly from French occupied territory alone, so that the available material can scarcely carry the 350,000 French workers ordered by Gauleiter Sauckel [for labor in the Reich].

The cars were requisitioned so quickly that not even loading them was possible, and they had to be set in motion to the Reich as empty trains.*

2.) At the moment, a large reorganization of all bodies subject to the transportation economy is in process, which largely consists of a takeover of the previously numerous bodies by the Reich Transportation Ministry.

This very recently and suddenly ordered arrangement will be completed only some days hence. Until that time, it is not even approximately possible to state whether sooner or later the transport of Jews to the foreseen extent can be carried out even partially or at all.

                              Dannecker
                              SS-Hauptsturmführer

* [Handwritten addition by Dannecker:] This office learned of this fact only today.

Document B.4. Note by Dannecker, 18 June 1942 [Memorial de la Shoah, Paris, Centre du documentation Juive contemporaine, XXVb-38]

IV J—SA 24   Paris, 18 June 1942
Dan./Ge.

    Re: Further Jewish transports from France

1. Note:
On 18 June 1942, SS-Obersturmführer Nowak (RSHA IV B 4) called and stated that despite the difficulties noted in our teletype Number 11291 of 16 June 1942, the Reich Transport Ministry is ready to accept large numbers of Jewish transports from France. It is therefore desirable to transmit immediately by teletype the departure stations in chronological order.

Because the number of Jews to be taken from the unoccupied area has not been clarified, I have offered to specify departure stations for about 40,000 Jews to begin with. As the military transport direction office in Paris has reported by telephone, the first three trains can roll from

Le Bourget-Drancy on 22 June 1942,
Pithiviers on 25 June 1942,
Beaune-la-Rolande on 28 June 1942.

                                 Dannecker
                                 SS-Hauptsturmführer

Document B.5. Correspondence between Albert Ganzenmüller, State Secretary in the Reich Transport Ministry, and Karl Wolff, chief of the personal staff of SS-Reichsführer Heinrich Himmler, 28 July–13 August 1942 (Nürnberg document NO-2207)

Dr.-Eng. Ganzenmüller   Berlin W8, 28 July 1942
State Secretary in the Reich Transport Ministry   Voßstraße 35
Acting General Director of the German National Railroad

SS-Obergruppenführer Wolf [*sic*]
Berlin SW 11
Prinz-Albrecht-Str. 8
—Personal Staff of the
Reichsführer-SS —

Much esteemed Party Comrade Wolf! [*sic*]

With reference to our telephone conversation of 16 July, I am informing you of the following report from my General Directorate of the Eastern Railroad (Gedob) in Kraków for your kind attention:

> since July 22, one train daily travels from Warsaw via Malkinia to Treblinka, each time with 5,000 Jews, as does a train twice per week with 5,000 Jews from Przemysl to Bełżec. Gedob is in constant contact with the Security Service in Kraków. It agrees to suspend transports from Warsaw via Lublin to Sobibór (near Lublin) as long as the repair work on this route makes transports impossible (roughly until October 1942).

The trains were arranged with the Commander of the Security Police in the General Government. SS- and Polizeiführer of the Lublin District, SS-Brigadeführer Globotschnigg [*sic*], has been informed.

Hail Hitler!

Yours sincerely,
[signed] Ganzenmüller

Führer Headquarters

Ba/Ms.
13 August 1942

To the
State Secretary in the Reich Transport Ministry
Acting General Director of the German National Railroad
Dr.-Eng. G a n z e n m ü l l e r
Berlin W 8
Voßstrasse 35.

Dear Party Comrade G a n z e n m ü l l e r !

Hearty thanks—also on behalf of the Reichsführer-SS [Heinrich Himmler]—for your letter of 28 July 1942. I have noted with special pleasure your message that for almost 14 days now a daily train travels to Treblinka with 5,000 members of the chosen people and that we are thus in a position to carry out this population movement at an accelerated pace. I have consulted with the participating agencies in order to assure a smooth execution of the entire undertaking. I thank you again for your exertions in this matter and beg to ask at the same time for your attention to these issues in the future.

With best greetings and

Hail Hitler!

W.

Document B.6. Note by Heinrich Himmler to Ganzenmüller, 20 January 1943
[Zentrale Stelle der Landesjustizverwaltungen, Ludwigsburg, USA, Bd. 1, 129–30]

Reichsführer-SS   20 January 1943
RF/V.
To State Secretary Dr.-Eng. Ganzenmüller, Berlin W8
Voßstr. 35
Teletype!

Esteemed Party Comrade G a n z e n m ü l l e r !

1.)

I confirm receipt of your letter of 12 January 1943.

The two cases of sabotage that I mentioned to you are the first of this sort that we can substantiate. However, indications are thickening that a special sabotage organization for the railroads is at work along with the usual partisans. I beg to ask you not to take lightly this information that I am quite purposefully passing on to you.

I am naturally agreeable to receiving a monthly copy of the summaries. Only the transmissions from here to SS-Obergruppenführer von dem Bach, who is the most important man out there [in the east], would take, in my opinion, too much time with the result that he always would get the statistics too late.

Now I come to you once more with an important question: A precondition for the pacification of the General Government, Białystok, and the Russian regions is the removal of all partisan helpers and suspects. A primary part of this activity is the removal of Jews. Likewise the removal of Jews from the west will be necessary, as we will otherwise have to reckon with an increase in the number of attacks.

In this, I need your help and support. I must have more transports if I want to settle these matters quickly. I well know how strained the situation is for the railroads and what demands are always being placed upon you. Nonetheless, I must direct this request to you: Help me and provide me with more trains.

H a i l H i t l e r !

Yours

signed H. H i m m l e r

2.) SS-Gruppenführer Müller
3.) SS-Obergruppenführer Pohl
4.) SS-Obergruppenführer Wolff
5.) Kommandostab SS
  copied for their information.

Document C.1. Railroad Direction Office Königsberg, Timetable Nr. 12, 7 May 1942
[Institut für Zeitgeschichte, Munich, Fb 85/II, 264–65]

German National Railroad
Railroad Direction Office Königsberg (Pr)   Königsberg (Pr), 7 May 1942
33 Bfp 9 Bfsv

Only for official use!

Timetable Nr. 12
Valid until 5 September 1942

To the offices and agencies on the route Platerow–Czerezcha to Wołkowysk, Operations Offices 1 and 2, Machines Office, Traffic Office, Car Distribution Agency, Train Direction, Bktr 5 and Main Railroad Station Białystok, HBD 33 and Operations Station Mitte in Minsk, Gedob 33 Kraków—according to special distributors —

For deporting resettlers, 1 special train per week will travel until further notice, Zug 30.9, with around 1,000 persons from Platerow (Vienna) via Czerezcha to Wołkowysk, Destination Minsk.

Arrive Platerow 10:11 [a.m.], depart 10:30 in Plan 92 247 B according to Timetable Book volume 22, Arrive Wołkowysk 16:35 [4:45 p.m.]. Further according to the timetable of Main Railroad Direction Mitte.

Traveling in the existing plan

Fr[iday]	Da 202 on 15 May		Fr[iday]	Da 210 on 10 July
"	Da 203 on 22 May		"	Da 211 on 17 July
"	Da 204 on 29 May		"	Da 212 on 24 July
"	Da 205 on 5 June		"	Da 213 on 31 July
"	Da 206 on 12 June		"	Da 214 on 7 August
"	Da 207 on 19 June		"	Da 215 on 14 August
"	Da 208 on 26 June		"	Da 216 on 21 August
"	Da 209 on 3 July		"	Da 217 on 28 August
			"	Da 218 on 4 September

Main Railroad Station Wołkowysk will report the arrival of one of these full trains immediately upon arrival to the National Railroad Direction Office Königsberg (Pr) Bfp 9 Telephone Nr. 483.

Locomotive and related equipment provided by Czerezcha workshops and station from Platerow to Wołkowysk, by Wołkowysk workshops and main station from Wołkowysk to Baranowicze.

In Wołkowysk, the occupants of the special train will transfer to cargo wagons. Covered cargo cars are to be ordered in timely fashion and made ready. To preserve order during the transfer, railroad guards and local police are to be called in, if necessary. Make sure of readiness to depart for Minsk at approximately 21:00 [9:00 p.m.] on the travel days.

The empty passenger trains are to be sent on the following day from Wołkowysk to Białystok as Lp Da 1202, 1203, etc. The Main Railroad Station at Białystok reports the arrival and the number of cars to National Railroad Direction Office Kbg [Königsberg] Bfp 9 immediately after arrival. Further use will be specially ordered in each case. Removal of wagons from these empty trains is prohibited.

signed Exner

Document C.2. Main Railroad Direction Office Mitte, Minsk, Timetable Nr. 40, 13 May 1942
[Institut für Zeitgeschichte, Munich, Fb 85/II, 270–71]

H B D Mitte
35 Bfp 5 Bfsv   Minsk, 13 May 1942

1) Kzl [German Chancellery] notice

Telegram message

T i m e t a b l e Nr. 40

To: Zmst, Hp, Bm, Bw, Brw, Zl, Bä, Mä, Vä von Wołkowysk bis Baranow-itsche bis Minsk Gbf [cargo yard], Czl, O11, L 20 Bfp, 1, 11, 12, 21, B 9, Vt1, Dez 33/34, 37, 21,7.
Informed National Railroad Direction Office Königsberg and Security Service Minsk
— each separately —

According to information from the National Railroad Direction Office at Königsberg, a special train (Train 30,9) with about 1,000 persons travels each week on Friday to Saturday from Vienna via Białystok–Barawnowitsche to the cargo yard at Minsk according to the following plan:

Arrive Wołkowysk at 16:35 [4:35 p.m.] according to the timetable of Direction Office Königsberg. Depart Wołkowysk to Baranowitsche until 12/13 June at 21:43 [9:43 p.m.] according to Timetable L 433. Arrive Baranowitsche at 2:44 [a.m.] from 19/20 June on. Depart Wołkowysk at 22:45 [10:45 p.m.] according to Plan M 435, arrive Baranwitsche at 5:21 [a.m.]. Depart Baranowitshe at 6:10 [a.m.] according to Plan M 135, arrive Minsk cargo yard at 11:50 [a.m.]. Train N 8111 follows from Stolpce.

Traveling in the existing plan are

Da 202 on 15 May	from Wołkowysk		Da 210 on 10 July	from Wołkowysk	
Da 203 on 22 May	"	"	Da 211 on 17 July	"	"
Da 204 on 29 May	"	"	Da 212 on 24 July	"	"
Da 205 on 5 June	"	"	Da 213 on 31 July	"	"
Da 206 on 12 June	"	"	Da 214 on 7 August	"	"
Da 207 on 19 June	"	"	Da 215 on 14 August	"	"
Da 208 on 26 June	"	"	Da 216 on 21 August	"	"
Da 209 on 3 July 3	"	"	Da 217 on 28 August	"	"
			Da 218 on 4 September	"	"

Each arrives at the Minsk cargo yard on Saturday.

The railroad station at Wołkowysk provides equipment consisting of cargo wagons for the resettlers and a second- or third-class passenger car. It also provides the locomotive and related equipment as far as Baranowitsche, then the station and workshops at Baranowitsche do so to the destination. The wagons return to normal service at the Minsk cargo yards.

Any missing parts of these arrangements can be reordered later.

Supplement for the Minsk cargo yard:

The Minsk cargo yard will report immediately after each arrival by telephone to Bfp 5, long distance number 13 or 69: the arrival, the number of axles of cargo and passenger cars, the number of people transported, and of these the number of children under the age of 10 and the number of accompanying personnel.

Main Railroad Station Direction Mitte
33 Bfp 5 Bfsv.

Z.V.
Distribution:

A. In-house distribution list for timetable records column 7 =	98
B. Routes 4 Sp 7 Lfd Nr 1-24	53
C. " 1 " 7 " " 20-62	102
D. Security Service Minsk	5
reserve:	42
	300

Document C.3. Karl Jacobi of Railroad General Operations Management East (Gedob) to National Railroad Direction Offices and others, 16 January 1943 [Zentrale Stelle der Landesjustizverwaltungen, Ludwigsburg, UdSSR, Bd. 108, Bl. 320–25]

German National Railroad   Berlin, 16 January 1943
General Operations Management East
        PW 113 Bfsv

Telegram Message!

To the National Railroad Direction Offices in
Berlin, Breslau, Dresden, Erfurt, Frankfurt, Halle (S),
Karlsruhe, Königsberg (Pr), Linz, Mainz, Oppeln,
East in Frankfurt (O), Posen, Vienna,
General Direction East in Kraków,
Reich Protector, Railroad Group in Prague,
GVD Warsaw, RVD Minsk,
informed: General Operations Management South in Munich, General Operations Management West in Essen
        — each receives 3 copies —

Subject: Special trains for resettlers in the period from 20 January to 28 February 1943

We are transmitting a list of the special trains for resettlers (Vd [ethnic Germans], Rm [Romanians], Po [Poles], Pj [Polish Jews], and Da [German resettlers, i.e., Jews being deported east]) in the period from 20 January to 28 February 1943 that were agreed upon in Berlin on 15 January 1943, and a plan for the circulation of the wagons to serve these trains.

The assembly of the trains is set forth in each case and to be obeyed. After each completed journey, the wagons are to be well cleaned, deloused if necessary, and made ready for further service after the end of this program. The number and category of the wagons is to be established after the final train journey, reported to us by telephone, and confirmed with an official service number.

signed Dr. Jacobi

GOM East Berlin
PW 113 Bfsv of
16 January 1943

LIST

of the special trains agreed upon in Berlin on 15 January
1943 for ethnic Germans (Vd), Romanians (Rm), Poles (Po),
Polish Jews (Pj), and Jews from the Reich and Western Europe
(Da) in the period 20 January to 18 February 1943
arranged by date of departure
[Lp = train traveling empty; W'hagen = Wilhelmshagen]

1	2	3	4	5	6	7
Date	Train Number	From	Departure	Destination	Arrival	Circulating Number
20 Jan	Vd 201	Kalisch	8:22	Ottersweier		106
	Da 101	Theresienstadt		Auschwitz		128
21 Jan	Lp 102	Auschwitz		Theresienstadt		128
22 Jan	Lp 202	Ottersweier		Andrzojow		106
23 Jan	Da 103	Theresienstadt		Auschwitz		128
24 Jan	Lp 104	Auschwitz		Theresienstadt		128
25 Jan	Vd 203	Andrzejow		Linz		106
	Rm 1	Gleiwitz		Czerenowitz		107
	Po 61	Zamocz	8:20	Berlin W'hagen	17:30	126
26 Jan	Da 105	Theresienstadt		Auschwitz		128
27 Jan	Lp 204	Linz		Kalisch		106
	Lp 106	Auschwitz		Theresienstadt		128
28 Jan	Lp 2	Czernowitz		Gleiwitz		107
29 Jan	Da 13	Berlin Moabit	17:20	Auschwitz	10:48	126
	Po 63	Zamosc	8:20	Berlin W'hagen	17:30	127
	Da 107	Theresienstadt		Auschwitz		128
30 Jan	Vd 205	Kalisch	8:22	Ottersweier		106
	Lp 108	Auschwitz		Theresienstadt		128
31 Jan	Lp 14	Auschwitz		Zamocz		126
1 Feb	Rm 3	Gleiwitz		Czernowitz		107

1	2	3	4	5	6	7
	Da 109	Theresienstadt		Auschwitz		128
2 Feb	Da 15	Berlin Moabit	17:20	Auschwitz	10:48	127
	Lp 110	Auschwitz		Myslowitz		128
3 Feb	Po 65	Zamosc	11:00	Auschwitz		126
4 Feb	Lp 4	Czernowitz		Ratibor		107
	Lp 16	Auschwitz		Litzmannstadt [Łódź]		127
	Lp 66	Auschwitz		Myslowitz		126
5 Feb	Pj 107	Białystok	9:00	Auschwitz	7:57	121
6 Feb	Pj 109	Białystok	9:00	Auschwitz	7:57	122
7 Feb	Pj 111	Białystok	9:00	Auschwitz	7:57	123
	Lp 108	Auschwitz		Białystok		121
8 Feb	Rm 5	Ratibor		Czernowitz		107
	Lp 110	Auschwitz		Białystok		122
	Lp 112	Auschwitz		Myslowitz		123
9 Feb	Pj 127	Białystok	9:00	Treblinka	12:10	121
	Lp 128	Treblinka	21:18	Białystok	1:30	121
10 Feb	Pj 129	Białystok	9:00	Treblinka	12:10	122
	Lp 130	Treblinka	21:18	Białystok	1:30	122
11 Feb	Pj 131	Białystok	9:00	Treblinka	12:10	121
	Lp 6	Czernowitz		Gleiwitz		107
	Lp 132	Treblinka	21:18	Białystok	1:30	121
12 Feb	Pj 133	Białystok	9:00	Treblinka	12:10	121
	Lp 134	Treblinka	21:18	Grodno		122
13 Feb	Pj 135	Białystok	9:00	Treblinka	12:10	121
	Lp136	Treblinka	21:18	Białystok	1:30	121
14 Feb	Pj 163	Grodno	5:40	Treblinka	12:10	122
	Lp 164	Treblinka	21:18	Białystok	1:30	122
15 Feb	Rm 7	Gleiwitz		Czernowitz		107
16 Feb						
17 Feb						
18 Feb	Lp 8	Czernowitz		Gleiwitz		107

GOM East Berlin
PW 113 Bfsv
of 16 January 1943

C i r c u l a t i o n P l a n

for the wagons to be used multiple times in service to
the special trains for ethnic Germans (Vd), Romanians (Rm), Poles (Po),
Polish Jews (Pj), and Resettlers (Da) in the period from 20 January to
18 February 1943

[Lp = train traveling empty; B = 2nd class passenger car;
C = 3rd class passenger car; G = covered cargo wagon]

1	2	3	4	5	6	7
Circulating Number	Supplier/ Rolling Stock	Date	Train Number	From	To	Number traveling
106	Pan 1 B 15 C	20–21 Jan	Vd 201	Kalisch 8:22	Ottersweier	700
		22–23 Jan	Lp 202	Ottersweier	Andrzcjow	
		25–26 Jan	Vd 203	Andrzcjow	Linz	500
		27–28 Jan	Lp 204	Linz	Kalisch	
		30–31 Jan	Vd 205	Kalisch 8:22	Ottersweier	700
107	Oppeln 1 BC 15 C 15 G	25–26 Jan	Rm 1	Gleiwitz	Czernowitz	600
		28–29 Jan	Lp 2	Czernowitz	Gleiwitz	
		1–2 Feb	Rm 3	Gleiwitz	Czernowitz	600
		4–5 Feb	Lp 4	Czernowitz	Ratibor	
		8–9 Feb	Rm 5	Ratibor	Czernowitz	600
		11–12 Feb	Lp 6	Czernowitz	Gleiwitz	
		15–16 Feb	Rm 7	Gleiwitz	Czernowitz	600
		18–19 Feb	Lp 8	Czernowitz	Gleiwitz	
121	Pan	5–6 Feb	Pj 107	Białystok 9:00	Auschwitz 7:57	2,000
		7–8 Feb	Lp 108	Auschwitz	Białystok	
		9 Feb	Pj 127	Białystok	Treblinka	2,000
		7–8 Feb	Lp 108	Auschwitz	Białystok	
		9 Feb	Pj 127	Białystok 9:00	Treblinka 12:10	2,000
		9 Feb	Lp 128	Treblinka 21:18	Białystok 1:30	

1	2	3	4	5	6	7
		11 Feb	Pj 131	Białystok 9:00	Treblinka 12:10	2,000
		11 Feb	Lp 132	Treblinka 21:18	Białystok 1:30	
		13Feb	Pj 135	Białystok 9:00	Treblinka 12:10	2,000
		13 Feb	Lp 136	Treblinka 21:18	Białystok 1:30	
122	Pan	6–7 Feb	Pj 109	Białystok 9:00	Auschwitz 12:10	2,000
	21 C	8–9 Feb	Lp 110	Auschwitz	Białystok	
		10 Feb	Pj 129	Białystok 9:00	Treblinka 12:10	2,000
		10 Feb	Lp 130	Treblinka 21:18	Białystok 1:30	
		12 Feb	Pj 133	Białystok 9:00	Treblinka 12:10	2,000
		12 Feb	Lp 134	Treblinka	Grodno	
		14 Feb	Pj 163	Grodno 5:40	Treblinka 12:10	2,000
		14 Feb	Lp164	Treblinka	Scharfenwiese	
123	Pan	7–8 Feb	Pj 111	Białystok	Auschwitz	123
	21 C	8 Feb	Lp 112	Auschwitz	Myslowitz	
126	Gedob 1 BC	25–26 Jan	Po 61	Zamocz 8:20	Berlin W'hagen 17:30	1,000
	16 C	29–30 Jan	Da 13	Berlin Moabit 17:20	Auschwitz 10:48	1,000
		31 Jan –1 Feb	Lp 14	Auschwitz	Zamocz	
		3–4 Feb	Po 65	Zamocz	Auschwitz	1,000
		4 Feb	Lp 66	Auschwitz	Myslowitz	
127	Gedob 1 BC	29–30 Jan	Po 63	Zamocz 8:20	Berlin W'hagen 17:30	1,000
	16 C	2–3 Feb	Da 15	Berlin Moabit 17:20	Auschwitz 10:48	1,000
		4–5 Feb	Lp 16	Auschwitz	Litzmannstadt	
128	Dresden	20–21 Jan	Da 101	Theresienstadt	Auschwitz	2,000
	21 C	21–22 Jan	Lp 102	Auschwitz	Theresienstadt	

1	2	3	4	5	6	7
	1 G	23–24 Jan	Da 103	Th	Au	2,000
		24–25 Jan	Lp 104	Au	Th	
		26–27 Jan	Da 105	Th	Au	2,000
		27–28 Jan	Lp 106	Au	Th	
		29–30 Jan	Da 107	Th	Au	2,000
		30–31 Jan	Lp 108	Au	Th	
		1–2 Feb	Da 109	Th	Au	2,000
		2 Feb	Lp 110	Auschwitz	Myslowitz	

Document D.1. Report by Police Assistant Waldbillig concerning provision of train equipment to transport Jews to and from Düsseldorf, 17 April 1942 [Zentrale Stelle der Landesjustizverwaltungen, Ludwigsburg, "Judendeportationen aus dem Reichsgebiet," appendix 30/1]

Düsseldorf, 17 April 1942

Report on discussions with the National Railroad Directorates in Wuppertal and Cologne concerning the provision of special trains and of train extensions for the transport of Jews to Düsseldorf and from Düsseldorf to the East.

I consulted with the National Railroad Directorate Wuppertal on 16 and 17 April 1942 regarding the provision of a transport train from Düsseldorf to the East. The train in question, which is supposed to carry Russian laborers from Brest to Cologne-Deutz and take 1,000 Jews on the return journey, has not left Brest yet. Another train from Russia to Hemer in Westphalia (Ru 7340) is now being provided, with the agreement of the Upper Operations Management East in Kraków and the main administration of the German National Railroad, for the transport of 1,000 Jews to Izbica. According to the prepared itineraries, the trains do not run to Trawniki, but rather Izbica, about 150 kilometers southeast of Trawniki. The Reich Security Main Office was informed by the Main Administration of the National Railroad that a train for Düsseldorf on 22 April 1942 stands ready and will leave Düsseldorf at 11:06 that day. The train will arrive in Düsseldorf on 20 or 21 April after complete cleaning and delousing. It will have 20 cars for people, but the kind of wagon is not definite, and since most trains from the east have the most varied types of wagons, a loading from the ramp in the livestock section of the station is not possible.

For transporting the 70 Jews from Wuppertal to Derendorf, train Pz [Personenzug = passenger train] 286 will be expanded at Steinbeck at 14:39 by one four-axle or two two-axle wagons. Arriving in the main station in Düsseldorf at 15:20. (The branch office in Wuppertal has been informed).

The 100 Jews from M[önchen]–Gladbach will be moved in two cars that will be attached to train Pz 2303 departing M[önchen]–Gladbach at 14:39. The train arrives at the main station in Düsseldorf at 15:21.

For 145 Jews from Krefeld, Pz 3167 from Krefeld at 15:46 to Düsseldorf Main Station at 14:17 [*sic*] will be extended with 2- to 4-axle passenger cars and one cargo wagon. The cargo car must be ordered from the fast freight office at the Krefeld station with the destination of Izbica.

The National Railroad Directorate in Essen is assembling a special train Da 152 (passenger cars) that will be extended with 2 cargo wagons for baggage. The cars similarly must be ordered in Essen with the destination of Izbica. The 3 cargo wagons will be brought to the ramp at the animal slaughter house, while the special train Da 152 and the individual wagons from Wuppertal, Krefeld and M[önchen]–Gladbach will be shunted to the ramp at Tussmanstadt.

(Waldbillig) Police Assistant

Document D.2. Guidelines for activated officials. Appendix to the urgent letter of the Secret Police, State Police Office Frankfurt am Main, 21 August 1942 [Kommission zur Erforschung der Geschichte der Frankfurter Juden, eds., *Dokumente zur Geschichte der Frankfurter Juden 1933–1945* (Frankfurt am Main: Kramer, 1963), 524–27]

Jews from the State Police district Frankfurt/M will be evacuated to the East. You are assigned to the execution of this action and to behave according to the provisions of these guidelines and the instructions delivered orally.

I expect that you will carry out this order with the necessary severity, correctness, and care.

Only full Jews will be deported. Stateless Jews will be treated as German subjects. The Jews will try with pleas and threats to make you soft or will be uncooperative. You must not let yourself be influenced in any way or be hindered in the execution of your duties.

These guidelines naturally can be only general. In individual cases, you therefore will have to decide what is necessary to guarantee an orderly process. In the event that a telephone is nearby, you can check back with the State Police Office Frankfurt/M. A table with the necessary telephone numbers is attached.

You will proceed as follows:

1. Enter the Jewish residences assigned to you at the appointed time. If the Jews refuse entrance and do not open, one of you should stay at the residence, while the other immediately informs the nearest police station.

   In the residence, call all the family members together and read to them the State Police decree, which should be handed to them with the Guidelines.

   The Jews must then stay in one room that you will assign to them. A second official stays with the family members the whole time. You direct your attention to the head of household.

2. Go with the head of household through the residence. If heated stoves are present, add no more fuel. In the case of slow burning stoves (tiled stoves or the like), the door should be screwed tight so that the flame goes out while you are still in the Jewish residence. When you leave the residence, the fire must be extinguished.

3. Then you and the head of household arrange for the packing of a suitcase or backpack. You must pay attention that only articles listed in the State Police decree are taken. You are responsible that valuables etc. that, according to the decree, may not be taken are not packed in the suitcase. Then you are to seal the suitcase. If consultation with

other family members is necessary, you accompany the head of household into the room where the other Jews are and let them say what other items should be packed. If necessary, leave the head of household there and go pack with the Jewess or another family member. Care must be taken in every case that the other family members remain under surveillance and are not alone for a moment.

4. The wool blankets that may be taken along must be rolled up or so folded that they can be transported without difficulty.

5. Go through the residence with the head of household (including cellars and attics) and establish what foodstuffs (perishable) and living inventory are in the residence. Collect these things with the head of household in the hall. Notify the NSV [National Socialist People's Welfare] and have the things taken away.

6. Valuable objects, savings books, stocks and bonds, jewelry and cash amounts that exceed the permitted allowance should be gathered by the Jew. The official is to accept these objects or valuables, to enter them in a list, and to pack them in a bag or envelope. The container should be closed and the first and last names, the locality, and the residence of the owner placed on the front side. The official and the Jew should check the listing for completeness and certify that with signatures. What is being taken away is also to be entered in the proceedings form.

   The attached proceedings record is to be filled out for every head of household or independent Jew and to be signed by the Jews and the official.

7. Have the Jew show you the personal papers that have to be delivered at the collection point.

8. All things (luggage, key to the residence) that you take away are to have durable labels that bear the name and precise address of the Jewish owner. These labels must be attached so firmly that they never fall off. The lettering must be clearly legible. The labels must be made while still in the residence and attached to the objects in question. In addition, each Jew must wear a sign around the neck, on which his name, birthday, and identity card number appear.

9. After you are finished with the inspection of the residence, attic, and cellar rooms, which—as I once more must emphasize—may be carried out only together with the Jewish head of household, then the official brings the Jews to the designated collection point.

   I point out that by this time everything in the residence must be settled. Pay particular attention that

   a) the pets (dogs, cats, song birds) have been handed over,

   b) perishable foods have been placed at the disposal of the NSV,

c) open fires have been extinguished,

d) water and gas lines have been shut off,

e) electric fuses have been screwed out,

f) the keys to the residence have been tied together with an attached label listing name, locality, and street address of the Jews, and

g) the Jews, as far as possible, have been searched before leaving for weapons, ammunition, explosives, and poison,

h) the property declaration has been filled out and signed.

10. After leaving the residence, the entrance is to be locked and sealed.

11. At the point of transfer in the collection area the objects and valuables taken into custody, the forms, guidelines, confiscation decrees, and the proceedings record are to be handed over.

12. Excesses are in every case to be prevented.

Document E.1. Confidential Report on the Evacuation of Jews to Riga on 11–17 December 1941 by Police Captain Salitter, 26 December 1941 [translated from the facsimile of the copy of the original in the Wiener Library reproduced in Gertrude Schneider, *Journey into Terror* (New York: Ark House, 1979), 195-210]

Düsseldorf, 26 December 1941

Confidential!
Report
on the evacuation of Jews to Riga
Transport Escort of 1 [officer]/15 [enlisted men]
from 11 to 17 December 1941

1.) The course of the transport

The transport of Jews scheduled for 11 December 1941 consisted of 1,007 Jews from the cities of Duisburg, Krefeld, and several smaller towns and rural communities of the Rhenish-Westphalian industrial region. Düsseldorf was represented by only 19 Jews. The transport was composed of Jews of both sexes and variable ages, from infant to 65 years old.

The departure of the transport was planned for 9:30 a.m., so the Jews were brought to the ramp for loading already at 4:00 a.m. However, the railroad could not assemble the special train that early, allegedly because of a shortage of personnel, and the boarding of the Jews could begin only at 9:00. Because the railroad insisted on the train departing as close as possible to the scheduled time, the boarding occurred in great haste. It was therefore not surprising that some wagons were overloaded (60–65 people), while others were occupied by 35–40 persons. This situation had adverse effects throughout the trip to Riga, since individual Jews tried repeatedly to get into the less crowded wagons. When time allowed, I changed car assignments in some cases, as mothers had become separated from their children.

On the way from the slaughterhouse [the collection point for the Jews] to the loading ramp, a male Jew tried to commit suicide by being run over by a tram. But he was caught by the streetcar's bumper and only lightly hurt. At first he pretended to be dying, but recovered during the trip, as he realized that he could not escape the fate of the evacuation. Similarly, an older Jewish woman left the ramp without being noticed—it was raining and very dark—and fled into a nearby house, undressed, and sat on a toilet. A cleaning woman saw her, and she, too, was led back to the transport.

Loading the Jews ended around 10:15 a.m. After being shunted around several times, the train left the cargo station at Düsseldorf–Derendorf in the direction of Wuppertal at 10:30 a.m., already delayed by one hour. After the last shunt, I realized that the guards' second-class wagon had been placed at the end of the passenger cars as the twenty-first wagon, instead of at the middle. Behind our car were the 7 cargo cars loaded with luggage. The false ordering of the escort car had the following disadvantages:

a) because of a faulty heating system, the steam pressure did not reach the rear wagons. In the resulting cold, the clothes of the guards could not dry (it rained during almost the entire trip), so I had to expect personnel losses due to illness.

b) I lost the ability to oversee the whole train. Even though the search-lights that we brought worked well, the guards had to go too long a way at each stop in order to supervise the wagons up front and often had difficulty getting back to the escort car when the train abruptly restarted. In addition, as soon as the train stopped at a station, the Jews tried repeatedly to make contact with the traveling public in order to get mail sent or water brought. As a result, I had to post two guards in a compartment of a passenger car at the front.

My complaints about all this were ignored in the departure station at Düsseldorf, and the train was dispatched with the comment that a rearrangement of the escort car was impossible because of the delay there, but could happen on the way.

The journey then proceeded according to schedule and passed through the following cities: Wuppertal, Hagen, Schwerte, Hamm. Around 6:00 p.m. we reached Hanover-Linden. Here the train stopped for almost an hour. I let some of the Jews have water and requested the rearrangement of the wagons. A promise was given to me, but at the last minute, no shunting locomotive was available. The station at Stendal would be given a message, so that my wish could be fulfilled there. The journey then led to Nisterhorst station. Here at 9:00 p.m. wagon 12 was found to have a burned out axle. The wagon had to be taken out of service and the Jews distributed among the other wagons because the station had no replacement. This action did not seem to please the sleeping Jews and unfolded at first with difficulty because of the unceasing rain and the darkness and because the train stood outside the station and beyond the platform, but was completed rather quickly by applying the appropriate pressure. The searchlights we brought proved very helpful during the reloading. Stendal station was reached around 11:00 p.m. Here the locomotive was changed and an empty third-class car placed at the head of the train. For reasons of expediency, I wanted to arrange the occupancy of that car only by daylight. Repositioning the escort wagon also was not possible here because the train was on the main track and had to leave immediately. Wustermark station was supposed to get a message, so that the repositioning could occur there.

Wustermark was reached on 12 December at 1:15 a.m. The station claimed not to have received a message from Stendal about the repositioning. So I was put off from station to station without my increasingly urgent request being fulfilled. Around 3:30 a.m. the train stopped for half an hour at the Berlin–Lichterfelde station. Here the senior management rejected a repositioning without giving reasons, noting that this could happen at the next stations if conditions permitted. The train now already had a delay of 155 minutes. The journey then was continued through Küstrin, Kreuz, Schneidemühl, Pirchau.

Around 10 o'clock I sent word from the Pirchau station to the Konitz station that the trains would have to stop there for one hour on a side track in order
    a) to fill the empty wagon with Jews,
    b) to provide the Jews with water,
    c) to reposition the escort car,
    d) to receive refreshments for the escort from the Red Cross.

The stop was approved. But just before Konitz, the train came apart because of overloading. The heating pipe broke apart, too. The train could be repaired in makeshift fashion and continue its journey to Konitz. It was reached at 11:10 a.m. I could carry out all my plans except repositioning my own wagon. At first this was promised to me, then the stationmaster explained that repositioning in the middle of the train was impossible because of the absence of a shunting engine and the unusability of the necessary track, but that he would move the escort car up front. I agreed given the prevailing circumstances. About five minutes later, he appeared again and declared that the train had to leave immediately and that a repositioning—in the meantime 50 minutes had passed—was no longer possible. The stationmaster's behavior seemed to me unreasonable, so I called him to account energetically and said I wanted to take my complaints to his oversight office. He told me that office was not open to me, he had his instructions and the train had to leave immediately because two trains from the opposite direction were expected. He even suggested that I clear a wagon in the middle of the train of Jews, put my troop in it, and put the Jews in the second-class escort car. It seems appropriate for an authoritative office to make clear to this railroad employee that members of the German Police are to be treated differently from Jews. I had the impression that he was one of those People's Comrades who still likes to speak of the "poor Jews" and to whom the concept "Jew" is alien. This train official managed even to let the train depart without me, while I had left it for two minutes to have the Red Cross station remove a foreign body from my eye. The locomotive driver stopped only because one of my guards intervened, and I could just reach the train. The claim that trains from the other direction were expected turned out to be threadbare, as in the ensuing journey our transport neither saw a train coming toward us nor were we overtaken at another stop by a train.

The two railroad officials (a conductor and a ticket collector) who had accompanied us since Pirchau could not comprehend the behavior of the official in Konitz. Their opinion as experts was that a repositioning during a one-hour stopover and on a sidetrack was easily possible, if only good will had been present. They had both offered their help in the repositioning and even already uncoupled the last wagon. At 12:10 p.m. the train left Konitz station. The journey led then through Dirschau, Marienburg, Elbing to Königsberg (Pr.) [Prussia]. Here the train was shunted around from 8:12 to 10:00 p.m. without the escort car being repositioned. In this station I received the news that a child was dying in car 17. I found out from the accompanying Jewish woman doctor that it was a 14-year-old girl with heart trouble brought on by her period. Around 10:10 p.m. the journey was continued. Shortly before Insterburg, the train broke apart again. Both parts had to be towed to Insterburg station, where the damaged wagon 15 had to be changed and the Jews loaded into a newly supplied one. Around 1:50 a.m., we went on to Tilsit. At that station near the East Prussian/Lithuanian border, in response to my renewed request in Insterburg, the escort wagon was moved to the front and finally got heating. The warmth did the escort good, as the uniforms of the guards were soaked through as a result of the rain that continued almost throughout the journey, but now could be dried out. At 5:15, we reached the border station at Laugszargen and 15 minutes later the Lithuanian station at Tauroggen. From here, the journey on to Riga normally should take another 14 hours. Because of the single track and the secondary priority of the train, there were often lengthy delays in the journey onward. At the Schaulen station (1:12 p.m.), the escort was sufficiently and well fed by the sisters of the Red Cross. We were served barley soup with beef. At Schaulen, Lithuanian railroad personnel cut off the lighting in the wagons with Jews. At the next station, I had the chance to let the Jews get water from a nearby source. The water in Lithuania can be enjoyed without boiling, but it is difficult to get because the sources are not always near the stations . . .

At 7:30 p.m. we reached Mitau (Latvia). Here the considerably colder temperature was noticeable. Snow flurries began and frost followed. Arrival occurred at 9:50 p.m. in Riga, where the train was held for 1 ½ hours. Here I learned that the Jews were not destined for the Riga ghetto, but were to be housed in the Skirotawa ghetto, 8 kilometers northeast of Riga. On 13 December at 11:35 p.m., after a lot of shunting around, the train reached the military platform at the Skirotawa station. The train remained unheated. The outdoor temperature was already 12 degrees below zero. Because a police reception unit was not present, my men continued to guard the train. The train was then handed over at 1:45 a.m. and guard duty taken over by 6 Latvian policemen. Because it was already past midnight and dark and the ramp was very icy, the unloading and transfer of the Jews to the ghetto 2 kilometers away was put off until dawn early on Sunday. My men were brought to Riga by 2 local police wagons and reached their quarters for the night at about 3:00 a.m. I was given lodgings at the guest house of the Higher SS and Police Command, Petersburger Hof, Schlossplatz. 4.

2) Stay in Riga

Considering that the men's uniforms, weapons, and equipment had become soaked and dirty on the way, I set aside 1 to 4 p.m. on 14 December for weapons cleaning and putting uniforms and equipment in order. Beforehand, I gave the men the chance to have a warm meal at a pub near their lodging. The authorities in Riga gave me the ration cards. I set the return trip of the escort for 3:01 p.m. on 15 December, as only one train per day for military personnel goes each day from Riga to Tilsit, and I had to give the 50,000 Reichsmark of "Jews money" that I had brought along to the treasurer of the state police early that morning.

The city of Riga is almost undamaged from the war. With the exception of blown up bridges over the Duna and a few shot-up houses nearby in the Old Town, I saw no further damage. Riga encompasses about 360,000 inhabitants, among them were some 35,000 Jews. The Jews were, as everywhere, leaders of the commercial world. Their businesses were closed and seized immediately after German troops marched in. The Jews were brought to a ghetto by the river surrounded by barbed wire. At present, there are supposed to be 2,500 male Jews in the ghetto who are used as labor. The others have been led off to another appropriate use or shot by the Latvians.

Riga is architecturally a very beautiful city and can compare itself to any city in the Reich. Transportation and economic life are well ordered. Clothing and food rationing was introduced a while ago. Foodstuffs are very cheap. An adequate lunch costs 50–75 pfennigs. As far as I could tell, the Latvian people are pro-German and most of them speak German. Often one could tell from the behavior of individuals that they remained loyal to Tsarist Russia. None of them want to be reminded of the Bolsheviks, however, because almost no family escaped a blood sacrifice during the Soviet occupation. They especially hate the Jews. Since the liberation, they have therefore participated very extensively in the elimination of these parasites. It seems incomprehensible to them, however, as I learned from Latvian railroad workers, why Germans bring Jews to Latvia instead of eliminating them in their own country.

The population may not be on the streets at night without a pass. In the recent past, there have been no more shootings. In the countryside, however, this is still the case. The instigators of unrest are partly old communists, partly also saboteurs parachuted in by the Soviets. To combat this rabble, adequate numbers of police battalions have been deployed. In Riga itself are located many staffs of supply units for the Army and the police.

Police troop units are not stationed in Riga.

3.) Return of the Guards

The return of the escort to Düsseldorf began on December 15 with the 3:01 p.m. train to Tilsit. The train was very crowded with soldiers on leave and arrived in Tilsit at 8:00 a.m. on 16 December. It needed 17 hours to cover 360 kilometers. After a stop of 3 hours, the journey continued without incident from Tilsit with regularly scheduled trains through Insterburg, Königsberg, Marienburg, Dirschau. On 17 December at 12:06 a.m. we reached Berlin. As soon as 12:30 a.m., we caught a furlough train from Berlin through Hanover, Hemm, and Dortmund and on to Düsseldorf at 1:00 p.m. The complete return journey from Riga took 46 hours; whereas for the journey out with a special train, we needed 61 hours.

4.) Experiences:

a) The food provided was good and sufficient.

b) Taking 2 blankets, cooking utensils, a gasoline cooker, warm clothing, furs, and felt boots did the men good and is also desirable for future transports.

c) Armament with pistols and carbines was sufficient, as attacks by partisans were to be feared in Latvia and Lithuania. In addition, in former

Russian regions, the armament of escorts with machine pistols, machine guns, and hand grenades is necessary.

d) The two hand-held search lights proved themselves well. I regard taking them as absolutely necessary for future transports. I used them from the train because they would have hindered the guards and made their use of weapons questionable.
Just as necessary is the equipment of the men with flashlights, replacement batteries, and candles as emergency lighting.

e) I have to praise the support of the Red Cross. With regard to the provision of refreshments the escort received every conceivable sort of support from the units we relied upon.

f) To supply the Jews with drinking water it is by all means necessary that the Gestapo and railroad agree on at least a one-hour stop per day at a suitable station. I found out that railroad officials, because of rigid schedules, are not willing to agree to the wishes of transport leaders. Usually the Jews have been moved around for at least 14 hours prior to deportation and therefore used up all the liquids they had taken along. If we do not supply them with water during the trip, they try to get out of the train at every opportunity, even when they are forbidden to do so, to get water either by themselves or by having someone get it for them.

f) Furthermore, it is also extremely important that the National Railroad have the trains ready on time, at least 3–4 hours before the scheduled departure, so that the loading of the Jews and their baggage can proceed in orderly fashion.
Above all, the Gestapo and the National Railroad must agree that the escort wagon (2nd class) be placed in the middle of the train from the very beginning of the transport. This is absolutely necessary for the secure surveillance of the transport. Otherwise the difficulties outlined in section 1 will result. In extreme cold, care must be taken that the heating equipment of the train is working.

g.) The men furnished for the escort gave rise to no significant complaint. Aside from the fact that I had to direct some of them to proceed more sharply against Jews who sought to defy my orders, the men all behaved well and did their duty properly. No cases of illness or unexpected incidents occurred.

signed S a l i t t e r
Captain of Police

Document E.2. Report of Police Reserve Lieutenant Fischmann on escorting a Jewish transport from Vienna to Sobibór, 14–20 June 1942, 20 June 1942 [Yad Vashem Archive, Jerusalem, 0-51/63/42-43; this translation in Christopher Browning, *Ordinary Men* (New York: HarperCollins, 2017), 27–30]

152nd Precinct   Vienna, 20 June 1942

Report of Experiences

Subject: Transport commando for the Jewish Transport Vienna–Aspangbahnhof to Sobibór, 14 June 1942.

The transport commando consisted of Reserve Lieutenant Fischmann as leader, two sergeants, and 13 reserve policemen of the 1st Reserve Police Company East. The duty of the transport commando began at 11 a.m. on 14 June 1942, at the Aspangbahnhof, in accordance with the prior telephone request of SS-Hauptsturmführer Brunner.

1. The loading of the Jews:

Under the direction and supervision of SS-Hauptsturmführer Brunner and SS-Hauptscharführer Girzik of the Central Agency for Jewish Emigration, the loading of the Jews into the special train waiting in the Aspangbahnhof began at noon and went smoothly. The guard duty of the transport commando commenced at this time. A total of 1,000 Jews were deported. The transfer of the Jews as listed occurred at 4 p.m. Because of a shortage of cars, the transport commando had to make do with a third- instead of a second-class car.

2. Trip from Vienna to Sobibór:

The train Da 38 was dispatched from Vienna at 7:08 p.m. on 14 June 1942, and traveled to Sobibór, not as scheduled to Izbica, via Lundenburg [Breclar], Brünn [Brno], Neisse [Nysa], Oppeln [Opole], Czestochowa, Kielce, Radom, Deblin, Lublin, and Chełm. Arrival in Sobibór on 17 June 1942, at 8:05 a.m. On arrival in Lublin at 9 p.m. on 16 June, SS-Obersturmführer Pohl was waiting for the train at the station and had 51 Jews capable of work between the ages of 15 and 50 removed from the train and taken to a work camp. At the same time, he gave the order to take the remaining 949 Jews to the work camp in Sobibór. Both lists of names, three wagons of baggage (with food supplies) as well as 100,000 zlotys were turned over to SS-Obersturmführer Pohl in Lublin. At 11 p.m. the train departed from Lublin for Sobibór. At the Jewish camp in Trawniki some 30 kilometers beyond Lublin, the three baggage wagons and food supplies were surrendered to SS-Scharführer Mayerhofer.

3. Delivery of the Jews in Sobibór:
At 8:15 a.m. on 17 June, the train drove into the work camp next to the Sobibór train station, where the camp commandant, First Lieutenant Stangl, took delivery of the 949 Jews. The unloading of the train began immediately and was completed by 9:15 a.m.

4. Trip from Sobibór to Vienna:
The return trip in the special train began around 10 a.m., immediately after completion of the unloading of the Jews, from Sobibór to Lublin, where we arrived at 2:30 a.m. on 18 June. No travel expenses were paid for this train. The trip continued from Lublin at 8:13 a.m. on 18 June by regularly scheduled express train to Kraków, where we arrived at 5:30 p.m. on the same day. In Kraków, we billeted with the Third Company of Reserve Police Battalion 74. On 19 June, this company handed out one day's rations to each of the 16 men. From Kraków, the return trip was again continued on the regularly scheduled express train at 8:08 p.m. on 19 June. Arrival in Vienna east train station at 6:30 a.m. on 20 June.

5. The transport commando stopover in Kraków:
The stopover of the transport commando in Kraków lasted 26 ½ hours.

6. Crossing the border:
The special train crossed the border between the Reich and the General Government on the outward journey on 15 June at 1:45 p.m., the regularly scheduled express train on the return trip at 12:15 a.m. on 20 June.

7. Provisions:
The men of the transport commando were provided with cold rations for four days. This consisted of sausage, bread, marmalade, and butter, but was nonetheless not sufficient. In Kraków the daily ration of the Third Company of Reserve Police Battalion 74 was good and sufficient.

8. Suggestions:
In future it will be necessary to provide the men of the transport commando with marching rations, because the cold rations do not keep in the summer months. The sausage—it was a soft sausage—was already opened and cut up when handed out on 15 June and had to be consumed no later than the third day because of the danger of spoiling. On the fourth day, the men had to be satisfied with marmalade, because the butter was also already rancid due to the tremendous heat in the train car. The size of the ration was also rather meager.

9. Incidents:
No incidents occurred either on the outward journey, the stopovers in the train stations, or the return trip.

(signed) Fischmann

Document E.3. Report of Police Lieutenant Westermann on two transports of Jews from Kolomea [Kołomyja] to Bełżec, 7–10 September 1942, 14 September 1942 [Zentrale Stelle der Landesjustizverwaltungen, Ludwigsburg, USSR Ord. No. 116, Bild 508-10; this translation in Browning, *Ordinary Men*, 31–36]

7/Pol. 24   Lemberg [Lwów], 14 September 1942

To: Commander of the Order Police in the district of Galicia, Lemberg
Subject: Jewish Resettlement

After carrying out Jewish resettlement actions on the 3rd and 5th of September in Skole, Stryj, and Khodorov, for which Captain of the Schutzpolizei Kröplein was in charge of the Order Police involved and which has already been reported in detail, the 7th Company of the 24th Police Regiment arrived as ordered in Kolomea on the evening of 6 September. I immediately contacted Kriminal Kommissar and SS-Obersturmführer Leitmaritz, head of the branch office of the Security Police in Kolomea, and First Lieutenant Hertel of the Schutzpolizei station in Kolomea.

Contrary to the experience in Stryj, the action planned for 7 September in Kolomea was well prepared and made easy for all units involved. The Jews had been informed by the above-mentioned agencies and the Labor Office to gather at the collection point of the Labor Office for registration on 7 September at 5:30 a.m. Some 5,300 Jews were actually assembled there at the appointed time. With all the manpower of my company, I sealed the Jewish quarter and searched thoroughly, whereby some 600 additional Jews were hunted down.

The loading of the transport train was completed about 7:00 p.m. After the Security Police released some 1,000 from the total rounded up, some 4,769 Jews were resettled. Each car of the transport was loaded with 100 Jews. The great heat prevailing that day made the entire action very difficult and greatly impeded the transport. After the regular nailing up and sealing of all cars, the transport train got underway to Bełżec at about 9:00 p.m. with a guard of one officer and nine men. With the coming of deep darkness in the night, many Jews escaped by squeezing through the air holes after removing the barbed wire. While the guard was able to shoot many of them immediately, most of the escaping Jews were eliminated that night or the next day by the railroad guard or the other police units. This transport was delivered in Bełżec without noteworthy incident, although given the length of the train and the deep darkness, the guard had proved to be too weak, as the commander of the transport guard from 6th Company of Police Regiment 24, who returned directly to Stanislawow [Stanisławów], was able to report to me in person on 11 September.

On 8 September, some 300 Jews—old and weak, ill, frail, and no longer transportable—were executed. According to the order of 4 September, to which I was first introduced on 6 September, concerning use of ammunition, 90 percent of all those executed were shot with carbines and rifles. Only in exceptional cases were pistols used.

On 8 and 10 September, actions in Kuty, Kosov, Horodenka, Zaplatov, and Sniatyn [Śniatyn] were carried out. Some 1,500 Jews had to be driven on foot marches 50 kilometers from Kuty or 35 kilometers from Kosov to Kolomea, where they were kept overnight in the courtyard of the Security Police prison with other Jews brought together from the region. Other than the Jews rounded up in Horodenka and Sniatyn, who had already been loaded onto ten cars at each location by the Security Police, another 30 cars were loaded in Kolomea. The total number sent to Bełżec on the resettlement train of 10 September amounted to 8,205.

In the actions in the area around Kolomea on 8 and 10 September, some 400 Jews had to be eliminated by shooting for the well-known reasons. In the great roundup of Jews to be resettled by 10 September in Kolomea, the Security Police loaded all Jews into the 30 available train cars despite the objections I expressed. Given the great heat prevailing on those days and the strain on the Jews from the long foot marches or from waiting for days without being given any provisions worth noting, the excessively great overloading of most of the cars with 180 to 200 Jews was catastrophic in a way that had tremendously adverse effects on the transport.

How densely the ten cars each in Horodenka and Sniatyn were loaded with Jews by the Security Police is beyond my knowledge. In any case, both transports arrived in Kolomea with completely inadequate guard, so that the barbed wire closing the air holes was almost completely removed. As quickly as possible, I had this train moved out of the train station in Kolomea and coupled with the 30 cars standing on the side track far from the station. The Jewish police [Ordnungsdienst] and members of the train station construction crew from Kolomea were employed until the onset of darkness to close up the insufficiently sealed cars in the usual regulation manner. A commando of one officer and fifteen men under the leadership of Captain Zitzmann was assigned to guard the parked resettlement train of 50 cars until departure and to prevent escape attempt. Given the already described strains on the Jews, the negative effect of the heat, and the great overloading of most of the cars, the Jews attempted time and again to break out of the parked train cars, as darkness had already set in toward 7:30 p.m. At 7:50 p.m. the guard commando of the resettlement train, with nine men under Corporal Jäcklein, arrived at the side track. Breakout attempts from the parked train could not be prevented in the darkness, nor could the escaping Jews be shot in flight. In all train cars the Jews had completely undressed because of the heat.

As the train left Kolomea on schedule at 8:50 p.m., the guard took up their stations. The guard commando, as initially stipulated by me, was divided into five men in a passenger car at the front and five men in a passenger car at the end of the train. On account of the length of the train and its total load of 8,205 Jews, this distribution proved to be unsuitable. Next time Corporal J. will arrange a distribution of guards along the entire train. Throughout the entire trip, the policemen had to remain in the cabooses in order to be able to counter the escape attempts of the Jews. Shortly into the journey the Jews attempted to break through the sides and even through the ceilings of certain train cars. They were partially successful in perpetrating this scheme, so that already five stations before Stanislawow, Corporal J. had to ask the stationmaster in Stanislawow by telephone to lay out nails and boards in order to seal the damaged cars as required by orders and to request the station guard to watch the train. As the train entered Stanislawow, the train station workers and the station guards were present to carry out the necessary repairs and in addition take over guarding the train.

The work took one and one-half hours. When the train subsequently re-sumed its journey, it was discovered at the next stop some stations later that once again large holes had been broken by the Jews in some of the train cars and that for the most part the barbed wire fastened on the out-side of the ventilation windows had been torn off. In one train car, the Jews had even been working with hammer and saw. Upon interrogation they explained that the Security Police had left these tools with them, because they could make good use of them at their next work place. Corporal J. made the Jews hand over the tools. During the further journey, at every stop, help was needed to nail up the train, because otherwise the rest of the trip would not have been at all possible. At 11:15 a.m., the train reached Lemberg. Because no relief for the escort commando arrived, the escort commando J. had to continue guarding the train until Bełżec. After a brief halt at the Lemberg train station, the train continued to the suburban sta-tion of Klaparov [Kleparow], where nine train cars marked with the letter

"L" and destined for the labor camp were turned over to SS-Obersturm-führer Schulze and unloaded. SS-Obersturmführer Schulze then had some additional 1,000 Jews loaded. About 1:30 p.m., the transport departed for Bełżec.

With the change of engine in Lemberg, such an old engine was hooked up that further travel was possible only with continuous interruptions. The slow journey was time and again used by the strongest Jews to press themselves through the holes they had forced open and to seek their safety in flight, because in jumping from the slow-moving train they were scarcely injured. Despite the repeated requests to the engineer to go faster, this was not possible, so that the frequent stops on open stretches became increasingly unpleasant.

Shortly beyond Lemberg, the commando had already shot off the ammunition they had with them and also used up an additional 200 rounds that they had received from army soldiers, so that for the rest of the journey they had to resort to stones while the train was moving and to fixed bayonets when the train was stopped.

The ever greater panic spreading among the Jews due to the great heat, overloading of the train cars, and stink of the dead bodies—when unloading the train cars some 2,000 Jews were found dead in the train—made the transport almost unworkable. At 6:45 p.m., the transport arrived in Bełżec, and around 7:30 p.m. was turned over by Corporal J. to the SS-Obersturm-führer and head of the camp there. Until the unloading of the transport around 10 p.m., J. had to remain in the camp, while the escort commando was used to guard the train cars parked outside the camp. Because of the special circumstances described, the number of Jews who escaped from this transport cannot be specified. Nonetheless, it can be assumed that at least two-thirds of the escaping Jews were shot or rendered harmless in some other way.

In the actions themselves for the period 7–10 September 1942, no special incidents occurred. The cooperation between the Security Police and the Order Police units involved was good and without friction.

(signed) Westermann
Reserve Lieutenant of the Schutzpolizei
and Company Commander

Document F.1. Postwar account by Hilde Sherman-Zander, Jewish survivor, of the transport from Düsseldorf to Riga, 10–14 December 1941 [Hilde Sherman-Zander, *Zwischen Tag und Dunkel: Mädchenjahre im Ghetto* (Frankfurt am Main: Ullstein, 1989), 29–34]

Transport to Riga: 10–14 December 1941

It was 10 December 1941. The train arrived in Düsseldorf in the afternoon. The doors were opened from the outside, and the police told us to leave our suitcases there, they would be brought later by truck. We were led on foot to the slaughterhouse. In an endless column, we marched there at dusk down the middle of the street. Not a soul was to be seen. But the window curtains moved, so that we knew that the population saw what was happening.

Then the elderly could no longer carry their baggage. They simply threw down their backpacks and handbags. When one looked back, the street was lined with stuff. The young people asked how they could help, but it was impossible to carry everything, all the more because the elderly soon had to be helped; they staggered and could hardly keep on their feet.

At the entrance to the slaughterhouse, young people were held back and then had to return the entire way and collect the scattered packages. My husband was among them.

I turned around and wanted to call something to him, when suddenly I received a blow in the back and fell down the narrow steps into the slaughterhouse. I will never forget this moment in my entire life: above on the steps stood P., a senior Gestapo official. With a face twisted in rage, he screamed down at me: "What are you waiting for? For a street car? They don't run for you ever again."

I was crushed. It was the first time in my life that a stranger struck me. My mother's slaps had all actually been squarely deserved. Thus I liked my mother just as much as before. The one time that my father slapped my face, I was deeply offended, my grandmother defended me, and in the end it hurt my father more than me.

This was the first time that a stranger touched me. And addressed me disrespectfully.

That was the beginning.

In Düsseldorf.

In Germany.

How will it continue? And in a foreign land?

The young people came back with the rest of the luggage. Then we were summoned alphabetically. Men and women had to give up their backpacks, which were ransacked by the Gestapo personnel.

To the right men were searched, women to the left. I entered a make-shift cubicle. A female official told me I had to undress. That took quite some time, because I wore a double layer of clothing under my coat: two jerseys, two pullovers, two blouses, three sets of underwear, one pair of ski trousers, and three pairs of socks in boots. Then I stood naked before a stranger.

For the first time in my life.

In Düsseldorf.

In Germany.

She told me to put my clothes back on and took away from me my bright blue angora pullover. Upon my leaving the cubicle, my backpack was returned to me. The writing case, made of dark blue and red velvet fabric that Ruth had given me as a farewell gift, was missing. She had made it herself. Along with the case, a fountain pen and mechanical pencil disappeared.

It was the first time in my life that I had been robbed.

In Düsseldorf.

In Germany.

Then we stood for the entire night in the slaughter house. The floor was wet, it was cold, and the dampness crept deep into our bodies. The chilblains in my feet began to hurt, but I did not dare take off my boots. Time and again we had to line up and on top of that were summoned alphabetically.

Babies and small children lay in the stone troughs of the slaughter house and cried the entire night, presumably from the cold.

Around four o'clock in the morning, we were led out. It was very cold, and we pressed against one another to mutually warm ourselves.

Then the Gestapo took our flashlights. Suddenly they beat a young man over the head with a rubber truncheon. He collapsed and remained lying on the ramp. He was still lying there three hours later, the first death of our transport.

In Düsseldorf.

In Germany.

As dawn broke, a train arrived. Our suitcases were loaded onto the last two cars. We entered the passenger compartments, eight people to a compartment: my parents-in-law, my sister-in-law Grete and her husband Alfred Cohnen, Alfred and Herbert Winter, Kurt and I. In the neighboring compartment, the Herzog family and six other people, all from Krefeld, squeezed in.

Toward nine o'clock the train slowly began to move. It was 11 December.

In our compartment it was awfully hot. We all fell half asleep, but that did not refresh us. Late in the afternoon we arrived in Berlin, at the Anhalter train station. We were not allowed to get out and fetch water.

The next morning we finally traveled farther. Almost all of us had taken off our shoes, because in the heat of the compartment our legs were swollen and inflamed up to the knee. Fanny, my mother-in-law, Herbert, and Kurt had fevers and terrible thirst. I was the only one in the compartment who had not dared to take off my boots out of fear that because of the chilblains I would not be able to put them on again.

Around midday the train stopped on an open stretch, just beyond Schneidemühl. The escorts flung the doors open and allowed us to get off and collect snow to melt for drinking water.

I was able to fill a batch of cooking pots with snow and hand them up to the compartment. I was glad for a brief moment to feel the fresh air and bright sun. What a stroke of luck that I had not taken off my boots! Thus we had drinking water in the compartment.

As soon as the snow collectors had climbed aboard, the train began to move once again. But in the opposite direction. Back to where we had come from! No one had any idea what that meant. At every turn we could see that both of the last two cars with our suitcases were still attached. What a comfort. . . .

Exactly two hours later we stopped once again on an open stretch. Only just after midnight did the train move again and now traveled through to Insterburg. There, we stopped at the station and were allowed to fetch water. At the end of the platform I saw a mailbox; I was able to mail a postcard that I had written to my parents, without being caught. People from other cars, whom we met by the water faucet, told us that the entire car full of children was unheated. Many already suffered from frostbite. And in our compartment, we almost died from the heat.

After the train had passed Memel, the setting changed visibly. Now we traveled through a dreary, monotonous, desolate winter landscape. Only now and then did a farmhouse appear, with deeply sagging roof practically crushed under the weight of the snow. Next to that a well. Often the inhabitants stood in front of their houses, muffled up in sheepskin coats, fur caps on their heads; the women wore thick headscarves, all had fur boots. An unbelievably depressing sight.

If that was the "Aryan" population of Lithuania, then what would become of us Jews? And far and wide only snow, snow, snow. . . .

As night fell, the train came to a standstill in a wilderness. Toward morning we traveled farther, only to stop once again two hours later. As it became light, we saw that we stood in a tiny station. No one had any idea where we were.

It was bitter cold. But the sun came up and bathed the entire landscape in a glistening, bluish light.

Around nine in the morning we heard the dogs barking, then we saw the SS arrive. They stationed themselves the length of the train on both sides. The doors were flung open: "Everyone out, but fast!"

Then we had to clean the compartments, with just our hands.

We were lined up in rows of five. Then Obersturmführer K. drove up with his adjutant "Gymnich" and his herd dog. K. struck a pose: "I am your ghetto commandant, of the ghetto in Riga, Latvia. Detachment—march!"

A man from our transport, a Mr. Meyer, who stood by his wife and carried his two children about three and five years old in his arms, approached K. and asked very politely: "Herr Kommandant, is it very far to the ghetto?"

Without answering K. raised his black walking stick with a silver knob and struck Mr. Meyer in the face with it. The two children fell to the ground, the herd dog pounced on Meyer and knocked him down. K., Gymnich and the dog turned around, got in their car, and drove away. Mr. Meyer's face was a bloody mass, both of his front teeth broken.

Our transport began to move; 1,079 human beings. Like an endless snake it wallowed through the endless snow landscape.

The population showed themselves in the doorways of the houses, very passive and hostile towards us. Only when someone could no longer carry his baggage, did they attempt to take it for themselves. The SS deliberately looked the other way.

Finally, in the distance, low, rundown wooden houses came into view, with an occasional stone house here and there. We were in the old town of Riga, in the so-called Moscow suburb. Everyone was very exhausted. The snow began to melt in the sun. Everywhere was frightfully slippery; ice like we had never experienced before. After a while the column turned sharply to the right, then over a small hill to the left onto a street empty of any human life. Then the gate closed behind us, and we had arrived at our destination: in the ghetto of Riga, Latvia.

The SS guard formed us up in rank and file. Finally, K. and Gymnich drove up. Two large board tables were set up in front of us, and K. barked: "Hand over all jewelry, watches and wedding rings likewise. Also furs!"

This gave rise to an immense confusion, during which I was able to shove my watchband higher up [my arm]. Our wedding rings were steel, we had no longer been allowed to buy gold ones.

Then order was restored and we were told:

The following is forbidden and punishable by death:
Jews may not possess any valuables.
Jews may not leave the ghetto.

Jews may not make contact with the civilian population through the barbed wire fence.
Jews may not barter.
Jews may not bear children.
Jews may not receive or send mail.
Jews may not . . . May not . . . And may not . . . Punishment by death . . . Punishment by death . . . Punishment by death . . .

SS men collected the things we had given up and loaded them onto trucks. The improvised tables were dismantled, and then the guard with K. and Gymnich drove away.

And we stood there with what we were wearing on our bodies. We never saw our suitcases, bedding, medicines, cookware again.

So we stood by the ghetto gate, always on the same spot. It began to get very cold. Suddenly people appeared out of the houses opposite us, with cups and a hot broth that was supposed to be coffee. They went up and down our rows, everyone received a cup full of hot liquid. What a pleasure to receive the first hot drink after five days!

The people were Jews deported from Cologne and Kassel, who had arrived on 10 and 12 December, just a few days before us. We began feverishly to ask them questions, but they were so remarkably quiet and reserved. "You will soon see what's happening," was pretty much the only thing we heard from them.

Suddenly the SS was there again. They drove us into the next cross street, then a couple of houses were counted off, and we were told: "Everyone here off the streets. Into the houses!"

We were speechless that all of us were supposed be accommodated there. Further orders followed:

Entering the street after sunset is forbidden. By sentence of death.
Crossing to the other side of the street is forbidden. By sentence of death.

We squeezed ourselves into a house that was two-storied, dark and sinister. But we had only a single wish: to stay together.

It was our first night in imprisonment, the night of 14 December 1941.

The nightmare began—only much worse than one could ever dream. And it lasted forever. After so many years.

It has never ceased.

Document F.2. Postwar account by Rudolf Reder, Jewish survivor, of his transport from Lviv (Lemberg) to Bełżec, 10–11 August 1942 [Rudolf Reder, *Belzec* (Oswiecim: Oswiecim-Brzezinka State Museum, 1999), 115–22].

In August 1942, we did not yet have a separate ghetto in Lwów [today: Lviv]. Several streets were designated exclusively for Jews. Thus it made up a Jewish district, consisting of a couple of streets set aside in the third district of Lwów, like Panienska, Waska, Ogrodnicka, Sloneczna Streets, and others. We lived here in anxiety and constant torment. Two weeks before the deportation, people everywhere were already talking about the coming misfortune. We despaired. We already knew what the word "deportation" meant. It was said that some worker had managed to escape the death crew at Bełżec, one of those who had built the chambers in the early days of setting up the death factory, and he talked about a "bathhouse," which in fact was a building intended as a gas chamber. He predicted that of the people forced to go in there, none would return.

It was also said that one of the Ukrainians employed in the killing of Jews had also told his girlfriend about what was going on at Bełżec. Appalled, she considered it her duty to spread the word and warn the doomed. This is how the news about Bełżec reached us.

The legend of Bełżec thus became a truth we knew about and that made us quake in fear. Many days before the tenth of August, terrified people were wandering the streets of the Jewish district helplessly, asking each other, "What can we do? What can we do?"

Then came the tenth of August. Early in the morning, guards blocked all the streets leading out of the district. Every few paces, Gestapo, SS, and Sonderdienst walked the streets in groups of five and six.

The Ukrainian militia were very helpful to them. Two weeks earlier, Generalmajor Katzman, the chief thug of Lwów and Eastern Malopolska, had already issued stamps[1] to some workplaces. Some employers also obtained stamps from the police commissariat on Smolki Square. There were few such "lucky ones." The majority, in their mortal fear, were searching for some means of salvation, of hiding themselves or escaping.

In the meantime, patrols had been searching house-by-house, every nook and cranny, for several days. Some Gestapo men acknowledged the stamps and some did not; those who did not have stamps and those whose stamps were not acknowledged were driven by force from their homes without being allowed to take even a shred of clothing or a slice of bread.

---

1. Stamps: certifications purporting to guarantee exemption from deportation, analogous to the "numbers" distributed in the Warsaw ghetto.

Next, the Gestapo herded crowds of people together and those who resisted got a bullet in the head. I was in my workshop, I was working, but had no stamp, so I locked the door and didn't answer even though I heard them finishing people off. The Gestapo broke the door down, found me in some hiding place, beat me over the head with a whip, and took me away. They packed us all into streetcars too tight for us to move or breathe and took us to the Janowska camp. It was already evening. They gathered us in a closed circle on a big meadow; there were six thousand of us. We were ordered to sit down and forbidden to stand, to move, or to stretch out an arm or a leg. A spotlight played on us from a tower; it was bright as day. Surrounded by armed thugs, we sat crowded incredibly close, all together, young and old, women and children of various ages. Several accurate shots rang out; someone had stood up; maybe he had wanted to be shot.

We sat that way all night. There was deadly silence. Neither the children or the women cried. At six o'clock in the morning, they ordered us to get up off the damp grass and form up in fours, and the long rows of the doomed marched to the Kleparow station. Gestapo and Ukrainians surrounded us in tight ranks. Not a single person could escape. They herded us onto the ramp at the station. A long freight train was already waiting just past the ramp. There were fifty cars. They began loading us. The doors of the freight cars had been slid open and Gestapo stood on both sides, two on each side with whips in their hands, beating everyone on the face and head on the way in. All the Gestapo were beating people. We all got welts on our faces and bumps on our heads. The women were sobbing and the children were crying hugging to their mothers. There were women with babies at the breast among us. Driven by the Gestapo who kept beating people ruthlessly, we stumbled over each other. The entrance was high, people had to climb up, pushing each other aside—we were in a hurry ourselves, we wanted to get it over with. A Gestapo man with a machine gun sat on the roof of each wagon. The Gestapo were beating people and counting off a hundred into each wagon. It all happened so fast that it took no longer than an hour to load several thousand people.

In our transport, there were many men, including employed ones with various kinds of work certificates, supposedly "safe ones," little children and bigger ones, young girls and older women.

They finally sealed the cars. Packed into a crowd of trembling people, we stood tight, practically one on top of another. It was stuffy and hot and we were close to madness. Not a drop of water, not a crumb of bread. The train moved at eight o'clock in the morning. I knew that the stoker and engineer in the locomotive were Germans. The train moved quickly, but to us it seemed very slow. It stopped several times, in Kulikow, Zolkiew and Rawa Ruska. The stops were probably needed for the coordination of rail traffic. During the stops, the Gestapo came down from the car roofs and prevented anyone from approaching the train. They did not allow us even a drop of water that people wanted to give, out of mercy, through the small grated window to those fainting from thirst.

We rode on. No one said a word. We were aware that we were headed for death, that nothing could save us; apathetic, not a single moan. We were all thinking one thing: how to escape. But there was no way. The freight car we were riding in was brand new, the window so narrow that I couldn't have squeezed through it. It must have been possible to pry the doors of other cars open, because we heard shots fired at escapees every few minutes. No one said anything to anybody, no one comforted the women lamenting, no one stopped the children from sobbing. We all knew: we were on our way to a certain and horrible death. We wished it was already over. Maybe someone escaped. I don't know . . . Escape could be attempted only from the train.

About noon, the train reached the Bełżec station. It was a small station. Little houses stood around it. The Gestapo lived in these little houses. Bełżec was on the Lublin-Tomaszow line, fifteen kilometers from Rawa Ruska. At the Bełżec station the train reversed from the main line onto a spur that ran another kilometer, straight through the gate of the death camp. Ukrainian railroad workers also lived near the Bełżec station, and there was a small post office. An old German with thick black mustache got into the locomotive at Bełżec—I do not know his name but I would recognize him in an instant; he looked like a hangman. He took command of the train and drove it right to the camp. It took two minutes to get to the camp. For the whole four months I would always see the same bandit.

The spur ran through fields. There was completely open space on both sides, not a single building. The German who had driven the train to the camp got down and "helped." Shouting and lashing out, he drove the people from the train. He himself went into each car and checked whether someone remained there. He knew all the tricks. When the train was empty and checked, he signaled with his flag and drove the train out of the camp.

The whole terrain between Bełżec and the camp had been taken over by the SS. No one was allowed to show himself there. Civilians who wandered in by mistake were shot. The train pulled into a yard about a kilometer long and wide, surrounded by barbed wire and iron fencing, one atop the other, two meters high. The wire was not electrified. You drove into that yard through a wide, wooden gate topped with barbed wire. Next to the gate stood a hut where a sentry sat with a telephone. In front of the hut stood several SS-men with dogs. When a train had passed through the gate, the sentry closed it and went inside the hut. That was when the "taking delivery of the train" took place. Several dozen SS-men opened the cars, screaming "los!" (Off!) They drove people out of the cars with whips and rifle butts. The cars had doors a meter above the ground, and all those being herded out, young and old, had to jump. They broke arms and legs during this, having to jump to the ground. Children hurt themselves, everyone fell dirty, exhausted and terrified. Aside from the SS, the so-called Zugführers [sic] were on duty. These were the supervisors of the permanent Jewish death crew in the camp, dressed normally without camp insignia. The sick, the old and the small children, all the ones who could not walk on their own, were placed on stretchers and set down at the edge of enormous dug graves. Gestapo man Irrman[2] shot them there, and then pushed them into the grave with the rifle butt. This same Irrman, a specialist in finishing off old people and small children, a tall Gestapo man, a handsome dark-haired man with a normal facial expression, lived, like the others, in Bełżec next to the station in a little house, all by himself and, like the others, had no family or woman.

He appeared in the camp early in the morning, spent the whole day there, and took delivery of the death transports. As soon as the victims were unloaded, they were assembled in the yard, surrounded by armed *askar*,[3] and here Irrman gave a speech. Everyone wanted to hear, hope dawned suddenly in us—"If they are speaking to us, perhaps we're going to live, perhaps there will be some sort of work after all. . . ."

Irrman spoke very loudly and distinctly. "Ihr gehts [sic] jetzt baden, nachher werdet ihr zur Arbeit geschickt" (Now you are going for a bath, and afterwards you will be sent to work). That was all. Everybody cheered up and was happy that they were going to work after all. They applauded. I remember his words repeated day in and day out, usually three times a day, repeated for the four months I was there. It was a moment of hope and delusion. For an instant, the people breathed easy. There was total calm. The whole crowd moved on in silence, the men straight through the yard to a building on which it was written in large letters: *Bade und Inhalationsräume* (baths and inhalation rooms). The women went some twenty meters further to a large barracks, thirty meters by fifteen. The women and girls had their hair shaved off in that barracks. They entered not knowing why they had been led there. The calm and silence lasted a moment longer. Later on I saw that only a few minutes later, when they were given wooden stools and lined up across the barracks, when they were ordered to sit, and eight

2. Irrman: SS-Scharführer Fritz Jierman, who was responsible for training and discipline among the Ukrainian crew of that place, numbering about sixty to eighty persons.

3. Refers to *askaris*, initially a term for nineteenth century native mercenaries in Germany's African colonies, subsequently used to refer to collaborators serving the Nazi occupation in Eastern Europe. [editor's note]

Jewish barbers, robots silent as the grave, approached them to shave their hair down to the scalp with clippers, the awareness of the whole truth hit them at that instant, and none of them and none of the men on the way to the chambers could have doubts any longer.

All of them, except for a few men selected as essential skilled workers, all of them—young and old, women and children—all of them were going to certain death. Little girls with long hair were herded in to be shaved, while the smallest girls with scant hair accompanied the men straight into the chambers.

Suddenly, without any transition between the hope and ultimate despair, there were laments and shrieks. Many women had fits of madness. Yet many other women went to their deaths coolly, especially the young girls. Our transport contained thousands of intellectuals and white-collar workers, many young men, but—as in all the subsequent transports—there was a majority of women.

I stood off to the side, in the yard, with the group picked out to dig graves, watching my brothers, sisters, acquaintances and friends being driven to their death. While the women were being herded forward naked and shaved, whipped like cattle to the slaughter, without being counted, faster, faster—the men had already died in the chambers. It took more or less two hours to shave the women, which is also how long it took to prepare for the murder and the murder itself.

Several dozen SS-men used whips and sharp bayonets to drive the women to the building with the chambers and up three steps to the gangway, where the *askars* counted 750 people into each chamber.[4] Women who balked at entering were bayoneted in the body by the *askars*, the blood flowed, and that is how they were driven in to the evil place. I heard the doors closing and the moans and screams; I heard the desperate cries in Polish and Yiddish, the bloodchilling laments of the children and the women, and then one joined, terrifying cry . . . That lasted fifteen minutes. The machine ran for twenty minutes, and after twenty minutes it was very quiet, the *askars* opened the doors from the outside, and I, together with the other workers picked out like me from the previous transports, without any tattoos or insignia—we went to work.

We dragged the bodies of people who had still been alive not long ago; we used leather straps to drag them to the huge, waiting mass graves, and the orchestra played during this. It played from morning to evening.

---

4. Initially, from March to mid-June 1942, three gas chambers housed in a wooden barrack functioned at the killing center. In the second half of 1942, a new concrete building was constructed, with six gas chambers able to hold a total of 2,500 people at a time.

RAUL HILBERG AND OTHER HISTORIANS OF THE GERMAN RAILWAY DURING THE NAZI ERA AND THE HOLOCAUST

Christopher R. Browning

On 29 November 1945, Lt. Col. Smith W. Brookhart Jr. interrogated Dieter Wisliceny in his cell at Nürnberg. Wisliceny had briefly been Adolf Eichmann's superior in 1937 and from 1940 to 1945 became a key member of Eichmann's "team" of experts dispatched by the Gestapo Jewish Desk in Berlin to various countries in Europe to implement the deportation of Jews to the killing centers in Poland as part of the Final Solution. Wisliceny was assigned to Slovakia, Greece, and Hungary. Wisliceny was among the first to give detailed, incriminating testimony about Eichmann and his key role, and he also briefly mentioned how the deportation trains from Greece had been procured. SS-Hauptsturmführer Franz Novak on Eichmann's staff sent a request to Otto Stange at the Reich Ministry of Transportation, a request that then went "through channels" to the area military transport command. As Jewish transports had "priority" (so Wisliceny claimed) over other freight movements, twenty-four trains were provided—averaging 2,300 Jews per train—to take some 55,000 Greek Jews from Salonica to Auschwitz between March and May 1943.[1] When Wisliceny gave his actual testimony before the International Military Tribunal on 3 January 1946, however, he presented an even more simplified and basically inaccurate version concerning the procurement of trains. His colleague from the Eichmann team in Salonica, Alois Brunner, had simply asked the transport command of the armed forces for the trains.[2]

Although Rudolf Höss would give relevant testimony on 15 April of that year, Wisliceny's testimony alongside that of Einsatzgruppe commander Otto Ohlendorf on 3 January marked the high point of the International Military Tribunal's focus on the Holocaust. But this provided no impetus for including the Transportation Ministry and the German Railway or Deutsche Reichsbahn as further subjects of investigation. And furthermore, the Minister of Transportation, Julius Dorpmüller, had died on 5 July 1945. His state secretary Albert Ganzenmüller made good his escape to Argentina (as did Eichmann). Franz Novak was living in Austria under an assumed name. And Otto Stange, the minor functionary who handled all charter trains on behalf of the Reichsbahn, from Alpine ski trips of the Strength through Joy program to one-way Jewish transports to Auschwitz, died in 1950. There were no obvious suspects to spur any further judicial investigation. And in reality, the Allies were interested in meeting with German railway men for two quite different reasons: to obtain information concerning the effectiveness of the bombing campaign and to obtain help in restoring the railway system in the postwar period.[3] No one envisaged this technical, logistical, and seemingly apolitical institution of German society as having been integral to Nazi criminality.

The earliest historians to attempt overviews of the Holocaust—Leon Poliakov and Gerald Reitlinger—likewise paid scant attention to the role of the Reichsbahn. In his chapter on deportations, Poliakov focused mainly on the coordinating role of Eichmann (including a mention of Franz Novak as his staff person responsible for obtaining trains), the horrors of ghetto liquidation in Poland, and the diplomatic and political complications of deportations from satellite and allied countries. The German Ministry of Transportation, the "thousands of trains" required for deportation, and the occasional suspension of deportations due to lack of transport were mentioned on one page.[4] Gerald Reitlinger twice mentioned the issue of rail transportation shortages, causing military opposition to deportations to Minsk in the fall of 1941 and delaying deportation from the Warsaw ghetto in the summer of 1942. In one footnote, based on Wisliceny's early affidavit, Reitlinger mentioned Eichmann and Novak's method for obtaining trains. But the historian erred in wrongly applying that description of train procurement for deportations from Greece to the General Government. In fact, a different procedure was used there.[5] Simply put, the role of the Reichsbahn remained unstudied and barely mentioned in the 1950s.

In the first edition (1961) of *The Destruction of the European Jews*, Raul Hilberg briefly made a series of points. First, restricting German Jews' use of rail transportation was part of the wider pattern of discrimination and segregation. In 1939, the Reich Transportation Ministry banned Jews from using dining and sleeping cars, but did not force them to sit in separate compartments. In 1942, the Security Police banned Jews from using dining and waiting rooms in train stations as well as using any public transportation, including local busses, street cars, and subways, without special permission.[6] Second, Hilberg noted that the actual Jewish transports were arranged between Eichmann and Franz Novak in the RSHA (Reichssicherheitshauptamt or Reich Main Security Office) and Novak's counterpart Minsterialrat Stange in the Transportation Ministry, and they were carried out by the Reichsbahn in sealed freight cars that were guarded by the Order Police (Ordnungspolizei or Orpo). The RSHA financed the participation of both Reichsbahn and Orpo through confiscated Jewish property, so that Jews ultimately self-financed their own transport to the killing centers.[7] Third, he noted the "crucial role" of the Ostbahn or confiscated Polish national railway taken over by the Germans. With 9,000 German personnel stretched thin, its 45,000 Polish employees must have done much of the work—including transporting 2 million Jews to camps—with little or no direct supervision.[8] Fourth, he offered a somewhat contradictory assessment concerning the priority of Jewish transports. On the one hand, he noted several occasions on which there were *Transportsperre* or bans on Jewish transports due to military demands, particularly in June/July 1942 and December 1942/January 1943. On the other hand, noting the uninterrupted flow of Jewish transports from the Third Reich in late 1941 when the German offensive stalled at the gates of Moscow, he concluded that "apparently military considerations" had not affected train allocations for the Final Solution.[9] At this point, however, Hilberg did not reflect more deeply on the significance of the role of the Reichsbahn for his overall interpretation of the Final Solution as a bureaucratic-administrative process involving all of organized German society.

In 1974, H.G. Adler, a survivor and sociologist who had published the first major study of the Theresienstadt ghetto,[10] published another remarkable book *Der verwaltete Mensch: Studien zur Deportation der Juden aus Deutschland.*[11] What might be awkwardly translated as "The Administered Man" was a more-than-a-thousand-page study of the administrative procedures that the Nazis employed to deport German and Austrian Jews (who together constituted fewer than 4 percent of all Holocaust victims). It was, in short, a study that embraced Hilberg's general approach of focusing on the bureaucracy of destruction but was devoted in excruciating detail to just one albeit very important aspect of the Final Solution. One chapter of this massive study constituted the first attempt to research the deportation trains: how they were scheduled, locally prepared, guarded, paid for, and reported on. On the basis of a handful of rare Reichsbahn documents recovered from the Minsk directorate, he noted that schedules of Jewish transports were planned several months in advance at periodic Reichsbahn scheduling conferences and all affected segments along the proposed routes were informed beforehand. For instance, on 8 August 1942, Dr. Engineer Jacobi of the *Generalbetriebsleitung Ost* in Berlin informed the

two other *Generalbetriebsleitungen* in Essen and Munich, the Ostbahn in
k and Riga of the fifty-one Jewish trans-
rious German cities and Theresienstadt
er 1942. He did likewise for thirty-four
een 20 January and 14 February 1943.
The first conveniently referred to Woł-
points instead of the nearby killing cen-
ka; the second openly listed Auschwitz

ments that each of the initial recipients
mptly passed on the necessary informa-
y. A 10 July 1942 communication from
Reichsbahndirektion Königsberg informed Minsk of the results of a planning conference in Bamberg—four incoming Jewish transports between 16 July and 8 August. On 15 August 1942, the Minsk directorate informed its local employees of eight incoming Jewish transports between 19 August and 7 October. Adler posed the question: "What did all the gentlemen of the Reichsbahn in Berlin, Breslau, Dresden, Erfurt, Essen, Frankfurt a.M., Halle, Karlsruhe, Königsberg, Krakau, Linz, Mainz, Munich, Oppeln, Posen, Prague, Warsaw, and Vienna think about the names Auschwitz and Treblinka?" A relevant question since all Jewish transports from Germany were designated "Da" to insure that they could be distinguished from other train traffic.[12]

Concerning the local preparation of transports, Adler made use of a then recently uncovered trove of surviving Gestapo files in Würzburg. Jews from surrounding villages were brought to Würzburg by bus or train, and then the Würzburg contingent was sent in separate train cars attached to regularly scheduled trains to the Langwasser assembly camp in Nürnberg (as were other Jews from the northern Franconian cities of Bayreuth and Bamberg). Thus, 200 Würzburg Jews were on the first Nürnberg transport to Riga in November 1941 and 170 on the fourth Nürnberg transport to Theresienstadt in September 1942. The Würzburg Order Police provided the officer and fifteen policemen who guarded the third Nürnberg transport, this time to Krasnystaw in the Lublin District in April 1942, as well as the second of two Nürnberg transports to Theresienstadt in September 1942. The costs incurred during the roundups and transfers from Würzburg to Nürnberg were calculated and billed down to the last pfennig. The reporting was equally thorough. For instance, for the April 1942 transport the Würzburg Gestapo sent reports to Eichmann in Berlin and to the commanders of the Security Police in Kraków and Nürnberg when the transport was underway; the guard commander confirmed arrival in Krasnystaw; and the Würzburg Gestapo chief then submitted a concluding report to his boss in Nürnberg.[13] And finally, Adler included in its entirety (and "without comment") the extraordinary "Salitter report" on the Jewish transport to Riga on 11–17 December 1941. That document had been found in the Düsseldorf archives.[14] [See Document E.1 in this book.]

Adler had based his chapter on a handful of Minsk railway directorate documents that he had found in the archives of the Institute for Contemporary History in Munich as well as on surviving Gestapo files from Würzburg and Düsseldorf. Raul Hilberg had been simultaneously pondering the same question. In a short personal account published in 1979, he recalled that after spending years examining "tens of thousands" of German documents, "I had become aware of a major gap in the unfolding panorama: there was a dearth of railway documents dealing with Jewish transports." In 1968, he visited Munich, where he saw the same Minsk documents that Adler had studied, as well as several other archives. But he concluded, "In the end, I was utterly frustrated." He could see that the trains were procured by the SS, but he could neither see "which railway office was processing these requests" nor "draw a diagram of the decision flow."[15]

Hilberg made a second trip "in search of the special trains" in 1976. His first stop was the Central Agency of the State Judicial Administrations for the Investigation of Nazi Crimes, located in a former women's prison in Ludwigsburg, north of Stuttgart. Founded in 1958 in the wake of the successful prosecution of the Tilsit Kommando in Ulm, it followed the method proven effective in that trial, namely of assigning teams to investigate various "crime complexes" to ascertain what crimes had been committed, what evidence in the form of documents and witnesses were available, and what suspected perpetrators still were alive and residing in Germany. At that point, the well-prepared investigations were turned over to the appropriate state prosecutors. Left to their own initiative, prosecutors had never had a starting point for investigating Nazis living within their jurisdictions except when occasional accidental encounters between former victims and perpetrators had led to accusations. At Ludwigsburg, Hilberg consulted additional railway documents that the Central Agency had obtained from Poland and the USSR. He visited the headquarters of the German Federal Railways in Frankfurt and the railway archive in Nürnberg, where it became clear that insofar as railway documentation had survived the war, most of it now was hoarded privately by past employees who had no intention of returning it to official hands.[16] And finally, Hilberg traveled to Vienna to look at the Austrian court records of the four trials of Eichmann's transport officer, Franz Novak, and to Düsseldorf to look at the court records of the trial of Transportation Ministry State Secretary Albert Ganzenmüller, who had returned from Argentina to Germany in 1955. The trial of Ganzenmüller had been suspended in 1973 due to the defendant's alleged poor health, but remarkably Hilberg received special permission from the judge to see the records of a trial not officially terminated until the following year.[17]

At the time, Hilberg was quite unsatisfied by the scholarly results of his trip and bitter about his overall experience in Germany. "I had started with a large gap in my knowledge and I was returning with a skeletal collection of texts and notes. The trip had netted very few documents. . . . There was a vast disproportion between what I had found and what was still missing in those archives." His pessimistic outlook was intensified by a bad experience with German customs, which reminded him all too much of the bureaucracy he had spent his life studying. He concluded that "I knew I was leaving Germany for good. No necessity I could imagine would bring me back."[18]

This assessment turned out to be wrong on two counts. First, the results of his research were not as meager as he portrayed. He quickly wrote up and published an article entitled "German Railroads/Jewish Souls" as a "special feature" in *Society*.[19] That article is included in this book. It may not have garnered much attention at the time, but it combined an astonishing achievement in detective work with deep reflection and insight that, taken together, constituted the vital breakthrough in the history of the German railways and the Holocaust. It was published in Germany alongside an extensive collection of documents and photographs under the title *Sonderzüge nach Auschwitz*, though of course the majority of such trains had other, less well-known, but equally lethal, destinations.[20]

And second, Hilberg in fact soon recanted his pledge never to return to Germany. In July 1982, he participated in an international conference held at the Sorbonne in Paris, where he delivered a paper also included in this book: "The Bureaucracy of Annihilation."[21] Here, he fit the German railroads into two wider contexts: first, that of understudied but indispensable agencies of the "machinery of destruction" (in this case both the German railway and the Order Police), and second, that of the bureaucratic essence of the Final Solution. After the conference, Hilberg crossed the border into Germany to work in the archives of the Central Agency in Ludwigsburg.[22] In May 1984, he returned to Germany yet again to participate in an international conference in Stuttgart and deliver his first public academic lecture in that country, on which occasion he was introduced by the mayor of Stuttgart, Manfred Rommel.[23] He returned frequently to Germany thereafter.

Hilberg's contributions emphasized the Reichbahn's participation in the Holocaust as a crucial example of the inherently bureaucratic nature of the Final Solution—non-political experts performing their jobs, motivated and measured by the efficiency with which they conducted themselves, not by the ends that their efficient performances served. For Hilberg, this kind of behavior was systemic and pervasive, and thus had little to do with individual personalities and their choices. In the following years, however, the authors of the next two books devoted to the topic shifted the focus to two key individuals—Albert Ganzenmüller and Franz Novak—and to the inadequacies of their postwar investigations and trials. The scholars were as much if not more concerned about what these cases revealed about the flaws of postwar society and failure of postwar justice in West Germany and Austria than about what these cases revealed about the Final Solution.

In 1985, West German journalist Heiner Lichtenstein published *Mit der Reichsbahn in den Tod*, based primarily on the records of the trial of Albert Ganzenmüller in Düsseldorf.[24] Quite contrary to the image of a naïve, apolitical technocrat whose expertise was misused by the regime to serve its evil ends, an image his defense cynically tried to cultivate at his trial, Ganzenmüller demonstrated that being both a committed Nazi from an early age and a highly educated and accomplished expert in his field were not mutually exclusive. Born in 1905, Ganzenmüller attended a Gymnasium in Munich. There, at the age of eighteen, he took part in the Beer Hall Putsch in 1923, for which he subsequently received the Nazi Party's coveted *Blutorden*. Passing the two highest levels of state exams in engineering and belonging to both the Nazi Party and SA, he entered a highly successful career with the Reichsbahn. In October 1941, he took over the Haupteisenbahnleitung Ost in Poltava, deep in occupied Soviet territory, and was credited with rescuing a collapsing rail system during the winter crisis of 1941/42. In June 1942, the thirty-seven-year-old Ganzenmüller was named State Secretary of the Transportation Ministry, with—Lichtenstein assumes—the crucial support of Himmler and Hedyrich.[25] Following his brief postwar internment by US forces and escape to Argentina, Ganzenmüller returned briefly to Germany in 1953 in an unsuccessful attempt to restore his pension. He then returned permanently in 1955 when prosecutions of Nazis in West Germany had reached their nadir and the Nazi-friendly Argentine regime of Juan Peron had been ousted.[26]

The major evidentiary threat to Ganzenmüller, cited in Gerald Reitlinger's then recently published book *The Final Solution*, was his correspondence with Himmler's adjutant, Karl Wolff, in the summer of 1942. Ganzenmüller had reacted positively to Wolff's urgent request on Himmler's behalf to provide trains for Jewish transports from the Warsaw ghetto and received Wolff's profuse thanks that five thousand "members of the chosen people" were now being sent daily to Treblinka. [See Document B.5 in this book.] A pre-trial investigation was opened in Dortmund in 1957 but stopped in 1959 when both Ganzenmüller and Wolff claimed that they had no idea about the purpose of these transports and the fate of the Jews in Treblinka. A second investigation in Dortmund in the 1960s, in which Lichtenstein described the investigating attorney as taking all of Ganzenmüller's testimony at face value and acting more like his defense attorney than a prosecutor, was likewise halted. Ganzenmüller was finally brought to trial in 1973, but only after the SPD justice minister of Nordrhein–Westphalia insisted on shifting the venue from Dortmund to Düsseldorf. After a few trial sessions, Ganzenmüller pleaded ill-health. The trial was suspended for four years, and then his case was declared permanently closed in 1977 on the grounds that Ganzenmüller would never recover sufficiently to stand trial.[27] What Lichtenstein could not know at the time his book was published in 1985 was that the allegedly ill Ganzenmüller would not die until 1996 at the respectable old age of ninety-one, having outlived the closing of legal proceedings against him on the grounds of ill-health by nearly twenty years! Lichtenstein noted that many of Ganzenmüller's colleagues successfully made the transition to the postwar Bundesbahn, and all managed remarkable amnesia and "reality-free apologetics" when questioned as potential witnesses for the Ganzenmüller trial.[28]

Like Hilberg, Lichtenstein found systemic problems that transcended Ganzenmüller's individual commitment to National Socialism. All railway men involved with the Jewish transports, from the highest to the lowest and with no record of refusal or dissent, continued to perform their duties and function well to the very end. Moreover, the Reichsbahn's business with the SS was very profitable. The company often provided trains and cars that were so old and decrepit that they could not be used for any other purpose, yet it charged the SS under the same fee structure as if it had provided charter trains for regular customers. The Reichsbahn was not blind to the fact that there would be no complaints forthcoming from the SS about substandard equipment to ship Jews on one-way journeys to the killing centers, just as the schedulers knew that there was no problem with the slow pace and long delays such transports experienced in giving way to virtually all other rail traffic.[29] Clearly, railway men at all levels knew precisely with whom they were dealing and what they were doing.

In 1994, Kurt Pätzold and Erika Schwartz contributed a study of Eichmann's transportation expert, Franz Novak, his postwar legal odyssey in Austria, and the implications of the role of the Reichsbahn in the Holocaust for our understanding of the Nazi era. Born into a comfortable family in southern Austria, Novak left school to apprentice as a typesetter and joined the Hitler Youth and SA as a teenager. In July 1934, he took part in the Nazi Putsch that attempted to seize control of Austria. Though successful in assassinating Chancellor Engelbert Dollfuss, the putsch quickly failed. Novak fled south over the Yugoslav border and was briefly interned before being allowed to leave for Germany where he served in the Austrian

Legion until returning to Austria during the Anschluss in March 1938. There he joined Eichmann's newly founded agency charged with accelerating Jewish expulsion from Austria, and subsequently followed Eichmann to Prague and then Berlin. When Eichmann became Heydrich's key adviser for Jewish affairs and also for ethnic cleansing in the "incorporated territories" of western Poland annexed to the Reich, Novak became his transportation expert. In order to organize transports of expellees from the "incorporated territories," Novak for the first time had to work with the Transportation Ministry, and in particular with Amtsrat Otto Stange, who was in charge of scheduling charter trains for the Reichsbahn. Beginning in October 1941, the frictionless cooperation of these two men resulted in transporting more than half a million Jews by train from the Reich, France, Belgium, the Netherlands, Italy, Croatia, Bulgaria, and Greece. In March 1944, Novak left his desk in Berlin to join the Eichmann-commando in Budapest, where he arranged for the 147 trains that took another 434,351 Jews to Auschwitz-Birkenau in the fifty-five days between 15 May and 8 July.[30]

After the war, Novak avoided internment by obtaining civilian clothes and false identification and working on a farm. He moved with his family to Vienna in 1947 and worked in a print shop, where he kept a photo of himself in SS uniform on his desk. By 1957, he was sufficiently confident of legal immunity that he successfully applied for the restoration of his Austrian citizenship (lost in 1934) under his real name. However, the successful Ulm trial (that had resulted in the conviction of all ten defendants of the Tilsit Kommando) and the founding of the Central Agency for the Investigation of Nazi Crimes in Germany in 1958, and the capture of Adolf Eichmann in 1960 rapidly altered the legal landscape. In January 1961, the state prosecutor in Frankfurt am Main issued a warrant for Novak. He was arrested in Vienna, and Austrian authorities decided to try him in Austria rather than extradite him to Germany.[31]

Novak was tried four times, during which he maintained the defense that he had merely been an insignificant clerk who only followed the instructions given him by others and that he had never known the fate of the Jews whom he arranged to transport to the east. In the first trial in 1964, he was convicted for his activities in Hungary but not for identical activities at his desk in Berlin. He successfully appealed and was acquitted in his 1966 trial on the grounds that he had no choice but to follow orders (*Befehlsnotstand*). The prosecution successfully appealed, and in a third trial, in 1969, the court rejected his dual claims of binding orders and ignorance of the Final Solution. Another successful appeal by Novak led to a fourth trial, in 1972, which upheld his guilty verdict but reduced his sentence from nine to seven years in prison. In light of his earlier pretrial incarceration of nearly six years, he was set free without serving further time, and he died in 1983. Kurt Pätzold and Erika Schwarz were particularly critical of the unexplained "judicial schizophrenia" of the Austrian courts, whereby Novak was acquitted of doing in Berlin what he was convicted of continuing to do in Budapest.[32]

Pätzold and Schwarz also rejected the notion that Novak's ability to procure trains throughout the war demonstrated that the Nazis were unequivocally more committed to killing Jews than winning the war. Insisting upon an approach more mindful of quantitative research than assumptions about ideological priority, they noted that during the war the Reichsbahn dispatched some 24,000–32,000 trains daily, and that with 1.1 million non-passenger train cars, some 30,000 stood idle each day. Even a considerable overestimate of ten Jewish transports per day would have claimed no more than 0.4 percent of German rolling stock. The success of the Final Solution, they argued, came not from an absolute priority imposed from above (Himmler requested rather than ordered trains from Ganzenmüller), but rather from numerous initiatives from below, as all too many Germans continually discovered how to adjust to every situation and overcome every obstacle. Moreover, they argued, one simply had to accept the difficult insight that an unbelievable crime could be committed with minimal material and manpower.[33]

Beginning in 1999, a steady flow of scholarship on the Reichsbahn during the Third Reich has expanded our knowledge considerably. Here the focus shifted away from the bureaucratic procedures for procuring Jewish transports that Hilberg had uncovered. Attention shifted to the broader picture of the institutional history, personnel, and political culture of the Reichsbahn. This also involved a temporal shift from the war years to the crucial early years of the Third Reich, when the Reichsbahn underwent a process of *Gleichschaltung*, "self-coordination" and accommodation with the Nazi regime, as well as a shift in emphasis from the Nazi technocrat and State Secretary Albert Ganzenmüller to the Reich Minister of Transportation and Reichsbahn General Director, Julius Dorpmüller. The foremost scholar in this regard was the prolific Alfred Gottwaldt,[34] but others made important contributions as well.[35]

Born in1869 and trained as a construction engineer, Dorpmüller made his initial mark building railways in China. Dismissed in 1917, he then made his way across revolutionary Russia back to Germany to participate in the last months of the war. In 1924, he was a member of the German delegation sent to London, negotiating the payment of reparations through Reichsbahn profits as part of the Dawes Plan. He was named General Director of the Reichsbahn in 1926 and carried out the modernization and rationalization of the company that enabled it to operate as a profitable business. Scorned on the right as a traitor for fulfilling Versailles Treaty reparations obligations through what it pejoratively called the "Dawesbahn," Dorpmüller was also attacked from the left as an enemy of the working class for cutting the railway workforce as an efficiency measure. By the late 1920s, however, he was valued as an apolitical expert of great accomplishment by German industry, foreign observers, and most of the Reichsbahn's own personnel.[36]

Hitler's assumption of power posed a different kind of challenge to Dorpmüller, and he soon revealed a different side of his personality. Showing himself a typical conservative nationalist product of the *Kaiserreich*, he desperately sought to preserve his job and at least some semblance of independence for the organization that he led, and he would do so through accommodation with the new regime. In the face of numerous demands and demonstrations by Nazi Party faithful for both his own removal and a sweeping purge of railway personnel, Dorpmüller publicly pledged the Reichsbahn's full support for the regime. He also agreed to the promotion of the Nazi and SA-man, Richard Kleinmann (deemed "acceptable" because he was also a qualified career railway man), to be in charge of personnel. Ultimately, a tacit deal was reached. Hitler kept Dorpmüller, who in turn presided over a thorough "self-coordination" of the Reichsbahn. One result of this deal was a rapid transformation of company personnel from top to bottom along three paths. First, the previous policy discouraging political activity was dropped, and current personnel—especially white-collar officials or *Beamten*—flocked to join the NSDAP (National Socialist German Workers' Party or Nazi Party). Second, in accordance with Hitler's decree for the "restoration" of the civil service, "non-Aryans" and those deemed politically unreliable were dismissed. Communists, Socialists, and union functionaries were especially targeted, as were Jews who did not enjoy one of the "Hindenburg exemptions" of World War I veteran status, wartime family loss, or pre-1914 appointment under the *Kaiserreich*. Some two-thirds of Jewish employers of the Reichsbahn who were initially shielded by one of these exemptions were invariably demoted to more obscure positions, only to be dismissed en masse in December 1935. Third, the Reichsbahn now engaged in a policy of preferential hiring and promotion of Nazis to fill new positions. The cumulative result was a quick and thorough nazification of Reichsbahn personnel.[37]

The dismissal of Jewish employees was only the first of many anti-Jewish measures adopted by the Reichsbahn in the 1930s. Books authored by Jews were banned from station bookstores, as were advertising placards of Jewish-owned firms from station displays. Contracts with Jewish-owned businesses were increasingly restricted, and the baggage of Jews traveling abroad was subjected to stricter handling to help the regime enforce the "flight tax" on emigrating Jews. Employees married to Jews were dismissed in 1937, and Jewish retirees were denied normal fringe benefits such as family passes for rail travel. In 1938, Jews were denied children's fares and student discounts, and railway employees were forbidden to shop at Jewish stores, patronize Jewish professionals such as doctors and lawyers, and even to socialize with Jews. And finally, in 1939, Jews were barred from dining and sleeping cars. And unlike so many other "coordinated" institutions in Nazi Germany, these measures were not produced by a "Jewish desk" or *Judenreferat* staffed by "specialists in Jewish affairs." They were the product of everyday procedures within the regular bureaucracy.[38] In short, by the late 1930s, the Reichsbahn as an institution had successfully isolated Jews from the lives of its employees and created an antisemitic corporate ethos.[39]

The "coordination" of the Reichsbahn with the Nazi regime extended far beyond its discriminatory anti-Jewish measures and nazifying personnel policies. In 1933, Dorpmüller ordered Reichsbahn personnel to use the "German greeting" and, following the death of Hindenburg in August 1934, to take a personal oath of loyalty to Hitler rather than to the German state. What had been a proudly autonomous and semiprivate institution transformed itself into a "tool of the dirigiste state."[40] State interests (initially political and economic but increasingly military and racial), not profit calculations, now determined decision- and policy-making. Make-work hiring, construction projects, and orders for new equipment were shaped by the regime's need for quick economic recovery. Massive price discounts (in the 50–75 percent range) were granted to the SS and SA, and especially for "special trains" for the group vacation opportunities of the Strength through Joy program as well as the transport of masses of supporters to party rallies. Once a profitable business, the Reichsbahn soon was incurring substantial deficits. Its legal corporate autonomy, which had originated in the now defunct treaty agreements of the 1920s, was abruptly altered in February 1937 when, in the name of restoring German sovereignty, the Reichsbahn was absorbed into the Ministry of Transportation as a government enterprise. Dorpmüller's reward for presiding over this transformation—in addition to the position of General Director of the Reichsbahn, which he retained— was to become the new Minister of Transportation.[41]

As noted, the Reichsbahn provided charter trains for group vacation and party rally trips for the party faithful on a regular basis, but in 1938 it began the ominous practice of one-way charter trains for the regime's racial victims. In October 1938, when the Polish government was on the verge of denationalizing Jews who held Polish passports but who had been long-term residents in Germany, the Nazi regime ordered their mass roundup and return to Poland. On 28–29 October, some 12,000–17,000 Jews were taken in charter trains to the Polish border. The Polish government blocked entry, and the expelled Jews were trapped in no-man's land between the borders. As Alfred Gottwaldt and Diana Schulle noted, this was the "paradigm" for the future cooperation between the Reichsbahn, German police, and other authorities for the deportation of Jews from the Reich. In the wake of the November pogrom less than two weeks later, some 25,000–30,000 adult male Jews were rounded up and sent to the Sachsenhausen, Buchenwald, and Dachau concentration camps. Once again, most of the victims were transported in some two dozen "special trains" provided by the Reichsbahn.[42]

The practice of shipping the regime's racial enemies on one-way charter trains intensified between 1939 and 1941. Eleven hundred German Jews were deported by train from Stettin to the General Government in February 1940, and 6,500 German Jews were dispatched from Baden and Pfalz to Vichy internment camps in southern France in October 1940. Some five thousand Jews from Vienna, Mährisch Ostrau, and Kattowitz had been sent to Nisko in the General Government in October 1939, and another five thousand Viennese Jews were deported to the General Government in February/March 1941. Most numerous of all during this period, more than 307,000 Poles and Jews were expelled from the "incorporated territories" of western Poland into the General Government between November 1939 and March 1941, again most of them by one-way charter trains.[43] The Reichsbahn was clearly in the habit of providing *Sonderzüge* for the massive deportation of the regime's racial victims long before the ultimate fate of Europe's Jews had been decided and the destination of the *Sonderzüge* became the Nazi killing centers of Chełmno, Bełżec, Sobibór, Treblinka, Maly Trostinez, and Auschwitz–Birkenau. As Alfred Gottwaldt noted, the role of the Reichsbahn as the "transporter of genocide" was prepared "step by step."[44]

These recent scholars of the Reichsbahn, the Nazi regime, and the Holocaust have also sought to deal with the issues of context and motivation. Klaus Hildebrand saw the fateful role of the Reichsbahn as an example of the dilemma posed by modernization and the "double face" of modern tyranny. The Reichsbahn combined logistical achievement and the perfection of modern technique on the one hand with the absence of any "ethical foundation" and a fateful neutrality toward good and evil on the other. The absorption of the Reichsbahn into the Nazi state and its essential contribution to the Holocaust were only the logical outcome of previous developments in the early 1930s. The enterprise's embrace of the Nazi regime was based on partial ideological affinity, adaptation to the spirit of the times, and crass opportunism.[45] Hildebrand also asked, how was it possible that "ordinary officials at all levels" (*gewöhnliche Beamten auf allen Stufen*) could participate in such an unprecedented crime? Here he turned to German political culture, particularly as exemplified among government officials, with its emphasis on order, bureaucratic procedure bolstered by apparent legality, service, discipline, and feelings of unqualified duty, obedience, and loyalty to the state. The time-honored traditions of German officialdom had been harnessed for the most monstrous purposes.[46]

For Alfred Mierzejewski, "indifference" was key. Dorpmüller "cared nothing about the fate of the Jews transported by his railway," and Reichsbahn personnel, like "most Germans," were "indifferent to the fate of the Jews, concentrating instead on their own personal affairs and the course of the war." Part of the problem was that the logistical demands of the Holocaust were so small compared to other rail traffic that they required little attention. But the wider problem again was one of political culture. "In a very real sense, the Deutsche Reichsbahn reflected the society that it served, obsessed with its internal processes, nationalistic, and common-weal-oriented, but ultimately, concerning overriding issues of human morality, narrow and stunted."[47]

Gottwaldt placed greater emphasis on antisemitism and the degree to which, step by step, Reichsbahn personnel had internalized and expressed the "Jew-hatred" of the regime. But this was combined with "callous" bureaucratic behavior and an obsession with efficiency that asked only how and not why. The result was a near total absence of resistance or even any indication of internal distress. Ultimately, Julius Dorpmüller more than Albert Ganzenmüller exemplified the wider attitudinal shortcomings of Reichsbahn personnel: competent, nationalist-conservative, dutiful, but politically blind. Dorpmüller was described as the "Hindenburg of the railroad" at his funeral oration in July 1945. Meant no doubt as praise, this characterization was unfortunately far more apt than the orator meant or realized. Like Hindenburg and Germany, Dorpmüller led the Reichsbahn down the path of national catastrophe, personal ignominy, and moral infamy.

Notes

1. Dieter Wisliceny affidavit C, 29 November 1945, in *Nazi Conspiracy and Aggression* (Washington, DC: US Government Printing Office, 1946), VIII, 606–19. On Wisliceny's complicated relationship with Eichmann and his many postwar testimonies, see Bettina Stangneth, *Eichmann before Jerusalem: The Unexamined Life of a Mass Murderer* (New York: Knopf, 2014), especially 283–85.

2. Testimony of Dieter Wisliceny, 3 January 1946 in IMT, 4:364–65.

3. Alfred Gottwaldt, *Dorpmüllers Reichsbahn: Die Ära des Reichsverkehrsministers Julius Dorpmüller 1920–1945* (Freiburg: EK-Verlag, 2009), 219–31.

4. Leon Polikov, *Harvest of Hate* (London: Elek Books, 1956), 144.

5. Gerald Reitlinger, *The Final Solution: The Attempt to Exterminate the Jews of Europe 1939–1945* (New York: Perpetua Edition, 1961), 91–92, 256–67. The role of Albert Ganzenmüller, the State Secretary of the Reich Ministry of Transportation, in obtaining

trains to begin the Warsaw deportation is mentioned, but he is mistakenly referred to as both Theodore and Teodor Ganzenmüller (257 and 508).

6. Raul Hilberg, *The Destruction of the European Jews* (Chicago: Quadrangle, 1961), 113, 117.

7. Ibid., 298, 354.

8. Ibid., 133–34, 311.

9. Ibid., 298, 313–14.

10. H. G. Adler, *Theresienstadt 1941–1945: Das Anlitz einer Zwangsgemeinschaft: Geschichte, Soziologie, Psychologie*, 2nd ed. (Tübingen: J.C.B. Mohr, 1960). English translation: *Theresienstadt 1941–1945: The Face of a Coerced Community* (New York: Cambridge University Press in association with the United States Holocaust Memorial Museum, 2017).

11. H.G. Adler, *Der verwaltete Mensch: Studien zur Deportation aus Deutschland* (Tübingen: J.C.B. Mohr, 1974).

12. Ibid., 441–46.

13. Ibid., 447–61.

14. Ibid., 461–65.

15. Raul Hilberg, "In Search of the Special Trains," *Midstream* (October 1979): 32.

16. Most important, Eugen Kreidler's *Die Eisenbahnen im Machtbereich der Achsenmächte während des Zweiten Weltkrieges* (Göttingen: Musterschmidt, 1975) referred to an extensive collection of privately held documents without mentioning anything about Jewish transports with which such documents would certainly have dealt.

17. I can say from personal experience that in early 1973 I was not allowed to consult the court records of Franz Rademacher, head of the Jewish desk of the German Foreign Office, after his third trial had been suspended due to poor health. I was denied because he was still alive in a prison hospital and the case might be resumed were he to recover. Once the case was closed due to his death later that year, I immediately received access.

18. Hilberg, "In Search of the Special Trains," 38.

19. Raul Hilberg, "German Railroads/Jewish Souls," *Society* (November/December 1976): 60–74.

20. Raul Hilberg, *Sonderzüge nach Auschwitz* (Mainz: Dumjahn, 1981). A second, slightly revised edition was published under the same title in 1987 by Ullstein.

21. Raul Hilberg, *Unanswered Questions: Nazi Germany and the Genocide of the Jews*, ed. Francois Furet (New York: Schocken Books, 1989), 119–33.

22. I know this because each of us traveled from the conference in Paris to Ludwigsburg and spent a week together working in the judicial records of the Central Agency.

23. Eberhard Jäckel and Jürgen Rohwer, eds. *Der Mord an den Juden im Zweiten Weltkrieg* (Stuttgart: DVA, 1985).

24. Heiner Lichtenstein, *Mit der Reichsbahn in den Tod: Massentransporte in den Holocaust 1941 bis 1945* (Cologne: Bund Verlag, 1985).

25. Ibid., 42–46.

26. Ibid., 10, 120–21.

27. Ibid., 121–30.

28. Ibid., 131–44.

29. Ibid., 34, 96.

30. Kurt Pätzold and Erika Schwarz, *"Auschwitz war für mich nur ein Bahnhof": Franz Novak—der Transportoffizier Adolf Eichmanns* (Berlin: Metropol Verlag, 1994), 11–51. Hungarian documents provide the figure 434,351 deportees; German documents 437,402.

31. Ibid., 57–68.

32. Ibid., 66–85.

33. Ibid., 86–95, 103–14.

34. Alfred Gottwaldt and Dianna Schulle, *Die "Judendeportationen" aus dem Deutschen Reich 1941–1945: Eine kommentierte Chronologie* (Wiesbaden: Marixverlag, 2005); Gottwaldt, *Dorpmüllers Reichsbahn*; and Gottwaldt, *Die Reichsbahn und die Juden 1933–1939: Antisemitismus bei der Eisenbahn in der Vorkriegszeit* (Wiesbaden: Marixverlag, 2011).

35. Klaus Hildebrand, "Die Deutsche Reichsbahn in der nationalsozialistische Diktatur 1933–1945," in *Die Eisenbahn in Deutschland: Von den Anfängen bis zur Gegenwart*, ed. by Lothar Gall and Manfred Pohl (Munich: C.H. Beck, 1999), 165–243; Alfred C. Mierzejewski, *The Most Valuable Asset of the Reich: A History of the German National Railway*, vol. 2 (Chapel Hill: University of North Carolina Press, 2000); Andreas Engwert and Susanne Till, eds., *Sonderzüge in den Tod: Die Deportationen mit der Deutschen Reichsbahn. Eine Dokumentation der Deutschen Bahn AG* (Cologne: Böhlau, 2009). Another recent book on the Reichsbahn and the Holocaust—Yaron Pasher, *Holocaust versus Wehrmacht: How Hitler's "Final Solution" Undermined the German War Effort* (Lawrence: University Press of Kansas, 2014)—will not be considered here, as it is devoted to a very different issue and approach, namely a counterfactual and speculative (and in my opinion not very persuasive) argument that had the Germans used the actual trains allocated as Jewish transports instead for just the right military purposes at just the right time and place in the course of the war, the military outcome would have been substantially altered in Germany's favor.

36. Gottwaldt, *Dorpmüllers Reichsbahn*, 8–65.

37. Mierzejewski, *The Most Valuable Asset of the Reich*, 1–9; Engwert and Till, *Die Deportationen mit der Deutschen Reichsbahn*, 29–33; Gottwaldt, *Dorpmüllers Reichsbahn*, 78–82; Gottwaldt, *Die Reichsbahn und die Juden*, 57–58, 76, 83–89, 137.

38. Gottwaldt, *Die Reichsbahn und die Juden*, 142–44, 159, 230–33, 240–41, 249, 313.

39. Engwert and Till, *Sonderzüge in den Tod*, 33; Gottwaldt, *Die Reichsbahn und die Juden*, 11.

40. Mierzejewski, *The Most Valuable Asset of the Reich*, 29.

41. Hildebrand, "Die Deutsche Reichsbahn in der nationalsozialistische Dikatur," 165–70, 200–208; Engwert and Till, *Sonderzüge in den Tod*, 34; Gottwaldt, *Dorpmüllers Reichsbahn*, 103–5; Gottwaldt, *Die Reichsbahn und die Juden*, 165.

42. Gottwaldt and Schulle, *Die "Judendeportationen" aus dem Deutschen Reich*, 26–30; Gottwaldt, *Die Reichsbahn und die Juden*, 363–86. For another argument connecting the deportations of 1938 with later deportations, see Wolf Gruner, "Von der Kollektivausweisung zur Deportation der Juden aus Deutschland (1938–1945): Neue Perspektiven und Dokumente," in *Die Deportation der Juden aus Deutschland: Pläne—Praxis—Reaktionen 1938–1945*, vol. 20 of *Beiträge zur Geschichte des Nationalsozialismus*, ed. Birthe Kundrus and Beate Meyer, 11–62, esp. 23–30. (Göttingen: Wallstein, 2004).

43. Christopher R. Browning, *The Origins of the Final Solution: The Evolution of Nazi Jewish Policy, September 1939–March 1942* (Lincoln: University of Nebraska Press, 2004), 36–72, 89–110.

44. Gottwaldt, *Die Reichsbahn und die Juden*, 402.

45. Hildebrand, "Die Deutsche Reichsbahn in der nationalsozialistischen Diktatur," 165–69.

46. Ibid., 241–43.

47. Mierzejewski, *The Most Valuable Asset of the Reich*, xiv, 162–64.

Bibliography

Adler, H. G. *Der verwaltete Mensch: Studien zur Deportation aus Deutschland*. Tübingen: J.C.B. Mohr, 1974.

————. *Theresienstadt 1941–1945: Das Anlitz einer Zwangsgemeinschaft: Geschichte, Soziologie, Psychologie*, 2nd ed. Tübingen: J.C.B. Mohr, 1960. English translation: Adler, H. G. *Theresienstadt 1941–1945: The Face of a Coerced Community*. New York: Cambridge University Press in association with the United States Holocaust Memorial Museum, 2017.

Browning, Christopher R., with contributions by Jürgen Matthäus. *The Origins of the Final Solution: The Evolution of Nazi Jewish Policy, September 1939–March 1942*. Lincoln: University of Nebraska Press, 2004.

Engwert, Andreas, and Susanne Till, eds. *Sonderzüge in den Tod: Die Deportationen mit der Deutschen Reichsbahn. Eine Dokumentation der Deutschen Bahn AG*. Cologne: Böhlau, 2009.

Gottwaldt, Alfred. *Dorpmüllers Reichsbahn: Die Ära des Reichsverkehrsministers Julius Dorpmüller 1920–1945*. Freiburg: EK-Verlag, 2009.

————. *Die Reichsbahn und die Juden 1933–1939: Antisemitismus bei der Eisenbahn in der Vorkriegszeit*. Wiesbaden: Marixverlag, 2011.

Gottwaldt, Alfred, and Dianna Schulle. *Die "Judendeportationen" aus dem Deutschen Reich 1941–1945: Eine kommentierte Chronologie*. Wiesbaden: Marixverlag, 2005.

Gruner, Wolf. "Von der Kollektivausweisung zur Deportation der Juden aus Deutschland 1938–1945: Neue Perspektiven und Dokumente." In *Die Deportation der Juden aus Deutschland: Pläne—Praxis—Reaktionen 1938–1945*, vol. 20 of *Beiträge zur Geschichte des Nationalsozialismus*, ed. Birthe Kundrus and Beate Meyer, 11–62. Göttingen: Wallstein, 2004.

Hilberg, Raul. "The Bureaucracy of Annihilation." In *Unanswered Questions: Nazi Germany and the Genocide of the Jews*, ed. Francois Furet, 119–33. New York: Schocken Books, 1989.

————. *The Destruction of the European Jews*. Chicago: Quadrangle, 1961; New York: Holmes & Meier, 1985; New Haven: Yale University Press, 2003.

————. "German Railroads/Jewish Souls." *Society* (November/December 1976): 60–74.

————. "In Search of the Special Trains." *Midstream* (October 1979): 32–38.

————. *Sonderzüge nach Auschwitz*. Mainz: Dumjahn, 1981.

Hildebrand, Klaus. "Die Deutsche Reichsbahn in der nationalsozialistische Diktatur 1933–1945." In *Die Eisenbahn in Deutschland: Von den Anfängen bis zur Gegenwart*, ed. Lothar Gall and Manfred Pohl, 165–243. Munich: C.H. Beck, 1999.

Jäckel, Eberhard, and Jürgen Rohwer, eds. *Der Mord an den Juden im Zweiten Weltkrieg*. Stuttgart: DVA, 1985.

Kreidler, Eugen. *Die Eisenbahnen im Machtbereich der Achsenmächte während des Zweiten Weltkrieges*. Göttingen: Musterschmidt, 1975.

Lichtenstein, Heiner. *Mit der Reichsbahn in den Tod: Massentransporte in den Holocaust 1941 bis 1945*. Cologne: Bund Verlag, 1985.

Mierzejewski, Alfred C. *The Most Valuable Asset of the Reich: A History of the German National Railway*, vol. 2. Chapel Hill: University of North Carolina Press, 2000.

Pätzold, Kurt, and Erika Schwarz, *"Auschwitz war für mich nur ein Bahnhof": Franz Novak— der Transportoffizier Adolf Eichmanns*. Berlin: Metropol Verlag, 1994.

Polikov, Leon. *Harvest of Hate*. London: Elek Books, 1956.

Reitlinger, Gerald. *The Final Solution: The Attempt to Exterminate the Jews of Europe 1939–1945*. New York: Perpetua Edition, 1961.

Stangneth, Bettina. *Eichmann before Jerusalem: The Unexamined Life of a Mass Murderer*. New York: Knopf, 2014.

HILBERG, THE RAILROADS, AND THE HOLOCAUST

Peter Hayes

In the now more than forty years since Raul Hilberg's path-breaking essay "German Railroads/Jewish Souls" directed scholars' attention to the role of the Reichsbahn in the murder of the European Jews, researchers have found few reasons to amend the account he provided. More detailed studies have added depth to our knowledge, but have not substantially altered his description of the scheduling, financing, and operation of the deportation trains.[1] Neither have subsequent researchers questioned the main point Hilberg emphasized: the managers of the Reichsbahn exhibited what he regarded as the central trait of modern bureaucracies, their treatment of means as ends, of performance as purpose, of fulfilling functions as the highest obligation. Knowing or being easily able to find out what they were enabling when they smoothly integrated the transportation of Jews "to the east" into routine operations, most railway executives scarcely gave a thought to the murders because they were someone else's responsibility.[2] "Normal procedures were employed . . . as if extreme decisions were not being made."[3]

But if Hilberg's chief findings have stood the test of time, his essay includes three tangential observations that have proved misleading. After noting problems that purportedly beset rail transport in the Third Reich during the war, Hilberg remarks, "yet throughout this time Jews were being sent to their deaths." A bit later, he comments, "Jewish transports were put together whenever and wherever there was a possibility of forming a train. They, too, had some priority." And, finally, Hilberg writes, "In the three-year period between October 1941 and October 1944 . . . despite difficulties and delays, no Jew was left alive for lack of transport."[4] The first statement ("throughout this time") makes no allowance for numerous and considerable ebbs and flows of deportation traffic even in the peak year of 1942, but especially thereafter. The second ("wherever there was a possibility . . . some priority") combines a tautology with an oxymoron. And the third ("no Jew") not only generalizes so broadly as to be unverifiable, but also overlooks the experience of most of the Jews of France between April 1944, when the Germans ordered all of them arrested, and the following August, when the Allies broke out of Normandy. Only three deportation trains moved in this period, as the Germans concentrated on defending against, first, the imminent, then the actual Allied invasion, and as bombing shattered the French transportation network.[5]

These errant formulations reflect an almost universal tendency in the early decades of Holocaust scholarship to overestimate the number and frequency of deportation trains, the amount of equipment they required, and the resulting deleterious effects on the German war effort. Despite a good deal of clarifying research since the 1980s, much of it by German scholars, some historians continue to lend credence to widespread misconceptions about these matters.[6] Although several recent survey histories of the Holocaust take pains to correct the record, their effect remains to be seen.[7] This volume provides an opportune forum to review what historians have learned about deportations of Jews by rail since Hilberg presented his pioneering essay.

Scholars' persistent misunderstandings about the deportation of Jews during the Holocaust result primarily from the mesmerizing effect of the huge death toll. Many historians reflexively suppose that massive results required a corresponding level of inputs. To kill 6 million people, half or slightly more of them after shipment to death camps, must have entailed, so the presumption goes, enormous outlays of personnel, equipment, and expense. We now know that this was false in almost every relevant respect.[8] The gases used (carbon monoxide and Zyklon) were cheap and in plentiful supply until after most of the killing had happened. Most of the death camps were ramshackle and jury-rigged, staffed by only twenty to thirty Germans supported by ninety to a hundred and thirty Eastern European auxiliaries, all of them more than paid for out of the booty taken from the victims. Even Auschwitz, eventually the biggest and most permanent killing site, depended initially on pilfered barbed wire, barter arrangements with I. G. Farben for crucial building materials, and refitting a powder magazine and two peasant houses as gas chambers.[9] And even at peak strength late in the war, that camp's German garrison came to roughly the size of a single Wehrmacht regiment.[10] Even the shooting units in the east represented little diversion from the front lines, as the Einsatzgruppen had only about three thousand members, and the Order Police battalions would have been assigned to occupation duties in any case, often consisted of people considered ineligible for the army, and were replaced increasingly during 1942 and thereafter by non-German *Schutzmannschaften.*

One of the most alarming aspects of the Holocaust is that its execution not only required tiny fractions of the Third Reich's personnel and resources, but also occurred in large part before these became stretched. After all, three-quarters of the Jews murdered in the Holocaust died before the German surrender at Stalingrad. By then, 90 percent of the Polish Jewish victims of the Nazi onslaught were already dead; two of the six death camps on prewar Polish soil had ceased operation, their missions to liquidate the Jews in their respective vicinities completed; and another two of the murder sites were winding down. So it was with the deportation trains: they made up a similarly small share of railroad traffic in the Nazi empire, and most ran before equipment shortages became pressing.

When Raul Hilberg wrote his essay in the mid-1970s, neither the total number of trains used to deport Jews nor the share of German rolling stock they required was well understood. Professor Wolfgang Scheffler had compiled the best available estimate on the former subject only a few years earlier in preparation for an abortive prosecution of Albert Ganzenmüller, the veteran Nazi who became State Secretary in the Reich Transportation Ministry in May 1942. Scheffler reckoned that 2,055 trains, carrying an average of 1,460 people each, had brought just over 3 million people to their deaths.[11] These figures remained the general baseline of understanding for many years because scholars of the Holocaust were understandably more concerned to find out how many people were deported from various locations over time than how many trains and wagons moved them.

Only in recent years have researchers tried to establish a comprehensive and reliable record of shipments to death camps. A pioneering effort of this sort, published in 2005, was Alfred Gottwaldt and Diana Schulle's compilation of the transports carrying Jews that left the Greater German Reich (including Austria, the Protectorate of Bohemia–Moravia, Luxemburg, and the territory annexed from Poland) between 1941 and 1945. The authors identified 414 transports of Jews to Theresienstadt and/or out of the Reich between 15 October 1941 and 15 April 1945, a span of forty-two months. This yields an average of almost exactly ten transports per month, one departing every three days. But many of these transports, especially in 1943–44, carried very few Jews and consisted only of one or two cars attached to the rear of regularly scheduled trains. Specially assembled trains (*Sonderzüge*) for deportations had to carry at least approximately four hundred Jews, the somewhat flexible threshold figure that triggered reduced fares per person.[12] The number of these dedicated transports in Gottwaldt and Schulle's itemization is 216, 193 of which departed between 15 October 1941 and 19 April 1943, and only twenty-three thereafter.[13]

The monthly average of significant departures is therefore almost eleven in the first eighteen-month period and fewer than one in the second period of twenty-four months.

At about the same time as Gottwaldt and Schulle's book appeared, Yad Vashem undertook to create a comprehensive and reliable online database of all deportations of Jews during the Holocaust.[14] That project is now largely complete with regard to the Greater German Reich (for which Yad Vashem provides higher totals than Gottwaldt and Schulle) and western and southern Europe, but not the General Government and parts of Eastern Europe. On the basis of Yad Vashem's findings and the other sources indicated, Table 5.1 presents my estimate of the number of large-scale transports involved in deporting Jews to their deaths from all of Nazi-con-

Table 5.1. Deportation transports, October 1941–October 1944[15]

Country	1941	1942	1943	1944	Total
Netherlands*	—	37	31	8	76
Belgium*	—	17	6	4	27
Luxembourg*	1	—	—	—	1
France	—	42	18	13	73
[Subtotal W. Europe	1	96	55	25	177
Slovakia	—	57	—	8	65
Italy	—	—	1	8	9
Hungary	—	—	—	147	147
Greece*	—	—	27	1	28
Croatia	—	5	2	—	7
Bulgaria	—	—	3	—	3
[Subtotal S. Europe	—	62	33	164	259
Germany*	27	59	17	2	105
Austria*	13	32	—	—	45
Protectorate*	13	96	19	15	143
Łódź*	—	73	1	18	92
[Subtotal Gr. Germany	53	260	37	35	385
Totals	54	418	125	223	821

Note: Trains to and from Theresienstadt are counted both times. *Sonderzüge only*, that is, trains assigned the prefix Da in the database and trains without that designation but destined to identifiable killing sites and large enough (at least approximately four hundred persons) to have been specially commissioned. Small transports consisting of wagons appended to regular train traffic are not included.

trolled Europe except the General Government and the occupied Soviet Union in the period from the onset of deportations in October 1941 to the termination of gassings at Auschwitz, the last operating death camp, at the end of October 1944.

My tabulation suggests that the deportations from most of Europe required 821 trains over thirty-six months, some twenty-three per month or fewer than one per day. Of these, almost half (47 percent) emanated from the Greater German Reich. The numbers also indicate that more than half of all transports rolled in 1942 at a rate of thirty-five per month or more than one per day, but that in this period, the Greater German Reich was the point of origin for more than three-fifths of the departures, the rest of Europe generating only thirteen per month or one every two days. And 1942 marked the highpoint of deportations from both inside and outside Germany, aside from the cataclysmic assault on Hungarian Jewry in 1944.

Because 1942 marked the apex of the Holocaust, Table 5.2 deploys the Yad Vashem findings, as well as other sources as indicated, to present an overview of the number of transports operating at the apogee of the killing, including trains in the German-occupied east to death camps. The statistics indicate that four to five trains departed per day over most of Nazi-controlled Europe while the murders were at their peak.

Table 5.2. Special trains departing to death camps at the apex of murder in 1942[16]

From	August	September
Netherlands*	8	7
Belgium*	6	5
France*	12	12
Germany*	6	11
Austria*	5	3
Protectorate*	5	15
Łódź*	0	7
Subtotal	42	60 = 102 over 61 days
Warsaw	25–27	10–11
Other origins to Bełżec	24	37
Other origins to Sobibór	0	0
Other origins to Treblinka	24	34
Other origins to Auschwitz	5	0
Subtotal	78–80	81–82 = ca. 160 over 61 days
TOTALS	120–122	141–142 = ca. 262 over 61 days

Now that we have a semi-complete picture of the number of transports dedicated to the murder of Jews, we can begin to calculate what proportion of German railway rolling stock this traffic entailed. Special trains (*Sonderzüge*) devoted solely to deportations varied considerably in length both by place and date of origin. From Germany, including Łódź, they usually consisted of about twenty passenger cars for deportees, plus or minus two to three wagons for luggage and guards; from Western Europe and Slovakia, the total number of cars was generally similar, but the use of freight wagons for the deportees was the norm.[17] By October 1942, the transports from Theresienstadt were becoming longer, including approximately twenty-seven cars for deportees and three more for goods and guards.[18] Late in the war, when the average number of deportees per transport more than doubled, more rolling stock may have been required. The trains from Hungary, however, were set at forty-five freight wagons, plus one car for guards, and at least one of the transports in March 1943 from Salonika in Greece consisted of forty-eight wagons.[19] In Poland and farther east, variation was enormous: the surviving records for 1942–43 show transports as small as sixteen to twenty-one cargo cars for deportees, plus one for guards, to as large as sixty freight wagons, plus or minus two for guards, during the great deportation from Warsaw.[20] In the summer of 1943, the final liquidations of the Lida and Minsk ghettos employed approximately twenty-three and twenty-nine freight wagons, respectively.[21]

Given all this variation, estimates of the equipment employed must be rough and calculated on the basis of averages. If one makes generous allowance and postulates that the average number of cars on each of the 627 trains from Western Europe, Greater Germany, and Slovakia works out to twenty-five and the corresponding figure for the forty-seven trains from Italy, Greece, Bulgaria, and Italy is forty, and then assumes that the Hungarian trains held to their planned strength of forty-five wagons, the total number of passenger and freight wagons used on the 821 known large-scale transports of Jews from outside the General Government (GG) and the occupied Soviet Union cannot have exceeded 24,317 (15,675 for the 627 trains from Western and Central Europe; 6,762 in the 147 Hungarian trains; and 1,880 from Southern Europe).

Compare these figures (as well as Scheffler's estimate of 2,055 trains and just over 3 million deportees, all told) to those in Table 5.3 concerning the carrying capacity of the German Reichsbahn as a whole in the period 1941–44. The total number of Jews transported to death (probably 2.5 million in 1942–43) is less than 0.5 percent of the more than 6.6 billion passengers the Reichsbahn carried in those years. Raise the number of victims to 3 million by the end of 1944 and estimate conservatively 2.5 billion Reichsbahn passengers that year, and the share of deported Jews drops to

Table 5.3. Reichsbahn carrying capacity, 1941–44[22]

	1941	1942	1943	1944
Total passengers carried (billions):	2.65	3.1	3.54	??
Total passenger cars (thousands)	70.5	72.4	71.0	??
Total luggage cars (thousands)	22.4	23.3	24.8	
Total cargo cars (thousands)	794.9	852.3	938.2	
Sum Total of all cars (thousands)	887.8	948.0	1034.0	
Trains operating daily (thousands)		—— 24,000–32,000 ——		
Average # of freight cars loaded daily (thousands)	153.7	147.7	158.4	141.5
Locomotives produced	1,900	2,600	5,200	3,500
Locomotives destroyed			6,600	
Cargo wagons produced	44,800	60,100	66,300	45,200
Cargo wagons destroyed			24,800	

0.3 percent. The total numbers of trains carrying Jews from outside of the GG and the occupied Soviet Union (821) and Scheffler's estimate of 2,055 total deportation trains represent infinitesimal fractions of the roughly 30 million trains (at an average of 28,000 per day) that ran during those three years. The 24,317 wagons used on all of the 821 documented trains over three years equal 16.3 percent of the average number of wagons loaded by the Reichsbahn every day in 1942–44 (149,200). Assume another 1,234 trains operated in the German East (to add up to Scheffler's total) with an average of forty wagons each, and the total additional wagons come to 49,400 or one-third of that average daily loading figure. Add both sets of numbers together (2,055 trains and 73,677 wagons), and the sums come to less than 10 percent of the number of trains operating daily in the Third Reich and less than 50 percent of the number of wagons loaded daily in German rail yards.

Another way of grasping how few of Germany's rail capacities became engaged in the Holocaust is to compare the number of transports of Jews to the number of trains involved in preparing major military operations. Even if Scheffler's total of 2,055 transports over three years turns out to be approximately correct—and the fragmentary statistics currently available suggest that the specially assembled trains to death camps from the General

Government and the occupied Soviet Union will add up to fewer than the 1,234 not currently accounted for—that figure scarcely stands comparison with the 16,000 trains (and 185,400 wagons) that deployed German troops and supplies to all fronts in August 1939 alone or the 33,000 trains used in preparation for Operation Barbarossa, as well as the 2,500 trains per working day sent to its staging areas between 22 May and 22 June 1941.[23]

The contextualization that these numbers provide leads inescapably to the conclusion that the deportation of the Jews did not represent a major challenge to the German railways or a significant drain on their resources during the apogee of death camp operations in 1942–43. As long ago as 1994, Kurt Pätzold and Erika Schwarz noted that even if ten deportation trains were in transit simultaneously on any given day in 1942, they would have constituted 0.4 percent of the trains in motion. The authors concluded pointedly, "None of the [transportation] problems that existed from the beginning to the end of the war were considerably or even appreciably worsened by the requirements of the RSHA [Reichssicherheitshauptamt or Reich Main Security Office] to achieve the 'final solution' or would have been solved by their absence."[24] More recently, Christian Gerlach established that the thirty-seven deportation trains running in the German Reich in April 1942 came to only slightly more than 1 percent of all the special trains created that month for various purposes, and much less than that proportion of the regular traffic in operation.[25] Such calculations are buttressed by an authoritative contemporary source. No less a figure than Albert Ganzenmüller told a conference at the propaganda ministry in Berlin on 14 July 1942 that the Reich was not short of rolling stock for its needs; in fact, he had 1.1 million freight wagons at his disposal, including those obtained from occupied countries, 140,000 of which rolled every day between Germany and the occupied East, and 30,000 of which stood idle daily for lack of cargo.[26]

The quantity of equipment required for deportations was even less significant than these numbers imply because the German railroad bureaucracy found several ways to contain the call on its resources. First, as Heiner Lichtenstein demonstrated long ago, the Reichsbahn scrimped on the equipment allocated for deportations. It often consisted of

> otherwise scarcely still usable cargo wagons . . ., including wagons that had been taken out of service [ausrangiert waren] . . . but then made operational again. . . . Non-watertight cargo cars were fine for Jews and gypsies, so were worn out locomotives with much reduced speed, because no fixed timetable had to be kept. . . . In this way the railroad secured revenues with trains and locomotives that otherwise had value only as scrap. . . . The railroad supplied cattle cars, indeed often old and rotted ones in which cattle or horses for the troops could no longer be transported.[27]

Even the passenger cars that the Reichsbahn deployed for German Jews were of similar quality. Jeannette Wolff described those that carried her from Dortmund to Riga in January 1942, as "decommissioned [*ausrangierte*], totally filthy fourth-class wagons . . . that could not have been used even one more time for transporting troops," not least because they were unheated and their toilets disgustingly full and frozen.[28]

Second, especially on recurrent routes such as Warsaw to Treblinka, the Reichsbahn set aside a limited, dedicated number of locomotives and cars so that one or more trains could shuttle back and forth repeatedly.[29] Already in early 1942, a single train traveling from the Galicia district to Bełżec and back sufficed to deport 200,000 people.[30] A conference at Eichmann's headquarters in Berlin in late September 1942 noted that five trains would soon run per day from various parts of Poland to Treblinka or Bełżec and back, each using cargo wagons that already had been allocated by the railroad directorate in Kraków [see Document A.2 in this book]; another gathering at the railroad management office for the East (GBL Ost) in Berlin on 1 January 1943 laid out the timetable for several "trains to be used multiple times" [*mehrfach zu verwendenden Wagenzüge*] between Theresienstadt or Białystok and Auschwitz or Treblinka [see Document C.3 in this book].[31] Two circulating trains, one to Bełżec and one to Sobibór, were all the Reich needed to empty the Izbica transit ghetto in late 1942.[32] Because the Nazi regime staggered deportations in the General Government, concentrating on different large ghettos in succession and phasing roundups in the small towns and countryside from district to district like a rolling barrage of artillery, the persecution machinery was able to reuse the same equipment over and over.[33] Moreover, this procedure had the added benefit of assuring that rail lines did not get congested. Even on the route through Malkinia, the junction where deportation trains turned off toward Treblinka, their average number per day during the murderous latter half of 1942 was only three, just 4 percent of the line's daily carrying capacity of seventy-two trains in that direction, and no impediment to the thirty to forty trains that each day supplied Army Group Center via that route.[34]

Still a third way of making sure that deportations did not drain the Reichsbahn's resources or clog its lines was through capitalizing on the return routes of otherwise necessary traffic. In 1942, fifteen to eighteen trains per day, each composed of twenty-seven boxcars and one passenger car for the escort, brought workers from the occupied East to Germany. These provided more than enough material to fill out the one to two transports of Jews that Tables 5.1 and 5.2 show left the Reich daily.[35] These "Russian trains/worker transports . . ., which are supposed to roll back empty into the General Government" constituted the only equipment that the Reichsbahn could make available to Eichmann in March 1942, but sufficed for his purpose.[36] Conversely, in November of that year, the Germans planned to add three trains per week to deport Jews from the Lublin and Radom districts of the General Government to Bełżec and Sobibór by redeploying wagons no longer needed to bring the Polish potato harvest west. [See Document A.2 in this book.][37] In 1943, the trains that carried Greek Jews to their deaths had supplied German occupation forces and lacked other return cargo.[38]

That the deportation of Jews depended on such expedients and workarounds reflected a fundamental fact: neither Adolf Eichmann nor his counterpart for deportations from within the General Government, Hans Höfle, and not even Heinrich Himmler had the power to demand or commandeer railway equipment.[39] They did not for a simple reason: the Holocaust did NOT have priority in the allocation of locomotives and wagons over other dimensions of the German effort, just as the trains used to deport Jews did NOT have priority over other traffic on the railways controlled by the Reich.[40] At both the policy (macro) and the operational (micro) level, the deportation of Jews was always subordinate to other, more pressing needs. That is why crowded and dilapidated freight cars carrying Jews repeatedly spent long hours shunted onto sidings while more important transports passed before resuming slow chugs toward death camps behind overtaxed and second-rate locomotives.[41] That is also why these trains got no better equipment.

Military considerations frequently impeded the flow of deportees, but the reverse happened seldom, if ever. Consider the following examples. Eichmann's initial transports of Jews to the Nisko "reservation" in southern Poland in late 1939 came to an abrupt end probably because Himmler needed the rolling stock for his demographic engineering effort farther north, but the Wehrmacht provided him with convenient cover by insisting that moving Polish prisoners of war and several German divisions in the opposite direction should take priority and by objecting to the creation of a large Jewish population near the then border with the Soviets.[42] In March 1941, the OKW (Oberkommando der Wehrmacht) directed the RSHA to suspend the shipment by rail of Bessarabian Germans into the Warthegau and Jews out of it because the Wehrmacht needed the rolling stock during the run up to the invasion of the Soviet Union.[43] Christian Gerlach has identified four other instances of military considerations prevailing over and blocking deportations of Jews: the termination of shipments from Germany to Minsk in November 1941 during the march on Moscow; the suspension of deportations in annexed and occupied Poland in the second half of June and the first half of September 1942 (which the Sobibór and Treblinka administrations used to build new, higher-capacity gas chambers) during the advance toward Stalingrad; the suspension of all deportation trains in the General Government from mid-December 1942 to mid-January 1943 during the siege of Stalingrad; and a longer interruption of transports from France at the turn of 1942/43, in part to reserve equipment for the movement of troops home on furlough for Christmas and back to their billets.[44] In a related vein, Yitzhak Arad has noted that the gas chambers at Bełżec and Sobibór did not operate at full capacity during the initial rounds of deportations from Polish ghettos from March to July of 1942 because the offensive in the southern USSR siphoned off rolling stock.[45]

David Cesarani maintains rightly that "no military action was ever suspended to ensure that the shipment of Jews to the gas chambers continued without interruption," but even by less stringent standards of measurement, the Holocaust did not undercut the German war effort, mostly because it was not allowed to do so.[46] The sort of high-quality railway equipment needed to move effective fighting forces—that is, air- and watertight, heated wagons for troops; flatbeds and other specialized cars to move artillery, armor, and fuel; and new, streamlined "war locomotives" and other types adapted to operating conditions in different war zones—was never used to transport Jews.[47] Moreover, as Gerlach's list notes, one of the most compelling examples of military considerations overriding deportation actions when clashes arose relates to events often cited as proof of the contrary. After ranking German officers on the Eastern Front in late 1941 objected to the use of trains to deport Jews to Minsk while soldiers on the fighting line were not receiving adequate supplies of food and ammunition, the deportations stopped, even though the connection between them and the supply bottlenecks was tenuous at best.[48] By autumn 1941, despite transportation tangles east of Warsaw, many German supply trains were getting through to the cities where Jews were being deposited, notably Riga (almost 350 miles from Leningrad) and Minsk (more than 400 miles from Moscow).[49] Indeed, these termini were chosen for Jews deported from Germany in part because any destination farther east would have interfered with military operations.[50] The catch was that very few supply trains were getting farther, because relatively few rail lines ran north and east from these cities, the Soviet retreat had devastated the fuel and water stations and locomotive exchange points along those few lines, weak roadbeds frequently collapsed under the weight of the German traffic, turnaround times at the railheads were laggard, and German train engines were poorly designed to withstand the increasingly extreme cold.[51]

Military considerations also were respected in another instance often cited as proof that murder had priority over the war effort, namely the massive deportations from Hungary between May and July 1944. The whole undertaking rested on a war-related justification: the need to obtain at least 100,000 Jewish slave laborers in order to make a reality of the Fighter Staff Program, the fantastical scheme to bury the Reich's principal arms-producing factories underground.[52] Moreover, the deportation trains took a northwesterly route to Auschwitz through Slovakia precisely to keep them away from the supply lines to the front in eastern Galicia.[53] And, finally, despite the enormous number of people involved, some 437,000 deportees, the allocation of equipment was trivial: 147 trains over fifty-five days, usually three but never more than six per day, accounting altogether for 1–2 percent of the daily railroad traffic in Hungary, and employing an infinitesimal 0.067 percent of the functioning locomotives and 0.1 percent of the rolling stock under the jurisdiction of the German Armaments Ministry at the time.[54] The relatively small requirements of the entire operation made no dent whatsoever in the Reich's ability to transfer two SS armored divisions swiftly from Ukraine to France during the second half of June 1944 while the Hungarian action was in motion.[55]

Another compelling testament to the priority of the war effort over the killing of Jews is the great decline in the frequency and number of deportation trains after Stalingrad that Table 5.1 documents. The sharp downturns in 1943 and continuing drop in 1944 (outside Hungary) resulted primarily from the diminishing number of Jews remaining for the Nazis to round up and the growing resistance in Europe to delivering Jews into Nazi hands, as Bulgaria and Romania reneged on promises to hand over their populations, and Vichy France's cooperativeness receded. But contributing to the decline was the reversal of Germany's military fortunes and thus the increasing concentration of rail resources on the Reich's struggle to survive. One can trace the effects in microcosm on the pace of deportations from the Netherlands. Having departed for Auschwitz every three to four days from July to November 1942, they left, now for Sobibór, only once every seven days from March to July 1943, then from either Vught or Westerbork, again to Auschwitz, at widening intervals thereafter.[56] The weekly rhythm allowed for the reuse of the same wagons, and a change after two transports of the departure day from Wednesday to Tuesday built enough time in the travel schedule for the trains to unload before the weekend and return in time for the next departure.[57]

What, then, is the state of the historical art today regarding Raul Hilberg's three claims mentioned at the beginning of this chapter? First, the deportation of the Jews was not continuous throughout the period 1941–44 but subject to numerous interruptions and a steep decline almost everywhere in Nazi-controlled Europe after 1942. Second, transports did not have priority of access to equipment except in unusual circumstances, such as France in mid-1942, when the German general who for a time commanded railroad traffic in that country shared the antisemitic convictions of his SS interlocutors [see Documents B.1 and B.2 in this book], or when a regime allied with Nazi Germany did, as in Slovakia in 1942 and Hungary in 1944. The Slovaks even provided the needed trains and paid the Germans to receive them.[58] Otherwise, deportations made do with relatively small reserves of frequently dilapidated equipment. Third, lack of transport contributed to the survival of many Jews late in the war, though it was not the principal reason why the lucky remnant lived to see the end of the Third Reich.

Of course, the relatively small scale of the Reichsbahn's role in the Holocaust has no bearing on an assessment of the conduct of the responsible railroad officials. They remain criminally complicit because they knew exactly what kind of "cargo" they were collecting one-way fares to carry to fixed destinations from which it never emerged. As Hilberg pointed out, the special prefixes assigned to the deportation trains' numbers referred explicitly to the category of people being carried, even if the abbreviation Da (*Deutsche Aussiedler*, or German Resettlers) used outside the General Government was more euphemistic than the letters Pj (*Polnische Juden*, or Polish Jews) used within it.

But an accurate appreciation of the relative scale of the railroad resources required for murder tells us something important about how and why the Reichsbahn could play its part effectively: because doing so was not very difficult until after the war turned against Germany. Participation entailed little equipment, much of it unusable or momentarily unused for other purposes, and transformed such equipment into revenue. Even after the tide of battle turned, enough such equipment remained to keep a slowing process going in fits and starts. Enough remained, even as the Third Reich collapsed in the first half of 1945, to ship tens of thousands of debilitated inmates from one concentration camp in Germany to another until liberation put an end to the ghoulish traffic.[59]

Notes

1. The principal additions to the literature in German since Hilberg wrote are: Heiner Lichtenstein, *Mit der Reichsbahn in den Tod* (Cologne: Bund, 1985); Kurt Pätzold and Erika Schwarz, *"Auschwitz war für mich nur ein Bahnhof": Franz Novak—der Transportoffizier Adolf Eichmanns* (Berlin: Metropol, 1994); Klaus Hildebrand, "Die Deutsche Reichsbahn in der nationalsozialistischen Diktatur 1933–1945," in *Die Eisenbahn in Deutschland*, ed. Lothar Gall and Manfred Pohl (Munich: Beck, 1999), 165–243; Alfred Gottwaldt and Diana Schulle, *Die "Judendeportationen" aus dem Deutschen Reich 1941–1945* (Wiesbaden: Marixverlag, 2005); Andreas Engwert and Susanne Kill, eds., *Sonderzüge in den Tod* (Cologne: Böhlau, 2009); Achim Jah, *Die Deportation der Juden aus Berlin* (Berlin: be-bra wissenschaft verlag, 2013); and a series of works by the late Alfred Gottwaldt: *Dorpmüllers Reichsbahn* (Freiburg: EK, 2009); *Die Reichsbahn und die Juden 1933–1939* (Wiesbaden: Marixverlag,

2011); and *Mahnort Güterbahnhof Moabit* (Berlin: Hentrich & Hentrich, 2015). In English, the major subsequent contribution is Alfred C. Mierzejewski, *The Most Valuable Asset of the Reich: A History of the German National Railway*, vol. 2: *1933–1945* (Chapel Hill: University of North Carolina Press, 2000).

2. On two railroad officials in Poland who opted out of participation in deportations to camps, without adverse consequences for their careers, see Mierzejewski, *Asset*, 2: 125–26.

3. Raul Hilberg, "The Bureaucracy of Annihilation," chapter 1 in this book, p. 11.

4. Raul Hilberg, "German Trains/Jewish Souls," chapter 2 in this book, pp. 29, 32, and 38. In the oft cited German book that contained a translation of Hilberg's essay, *Sonderzüge nach Auschwitz* (Frankfurt am Main: Ullstein, 1987), the sentences and the place where they appear are: "Die ganze Zeit über wurden die Juden in den Tod transportiert," 52; "aber die Judentransporte fanden statt, wo und wann auch immer sich die Möglichkeit zur Zusammenstellung eines Zuges ergab. Auch sie waren dringlich!," 63; "trotz aller Probleme und Verzögerungen blieb in der ganzen Zeit kein einziger Jude wegen Transportschwierigkeiten am Leben," 89.

5. Richard Overy, *The Bombers and the Bombed: Allied Air War over Europe, 1940–1945* (New York: Viking, 2013), 390–94; Williamson Murray and Allan R. Millett, *A War to Be Won* (Cambridge, MA: Harvard University Press, 2000), 413–16.

6. See note 1 for the titles that have provided the clarifying research. In fairness, I should note that even though Lichtenstein's evidence and argument overwhelmingly contradict the notion that deportations took priority over and interfered with the German war effort, even he occasionally relapsed, see *In den Tod*, 48. For continuations of the prevalent misconception, see Gerhard Weinberg, *A World at Arms: A Global History of World War II* (New York: Cambridge University Press, 1994), 293; Doris Bergen, *War and Genocide: A Concise History of the Holocaust*, 3rd ed. (Lanham, MD: Rowman & Littlefield, 2016), 279; Julia S. Torrie, *"For Their Own Good": Civilian Evacuations in Germany and France, 1939–1945* (New York: Berghahn, 2010), 137; and Yaron Pasher, *Holocaust versus Wehrmacht: How Hitler's "Final Solution" Undermined the German War Effort* (Lawrence: University Press of Kansas, 2014), passim. I outlined some of the shortcomings of Pasher's misleading and unreliable book in a review for *Holocaust and Genocide Studies* 29 (2015): 278–81. Many (but by no means all) of these deficiencies stem, the author's notes and bibliography indicate, from his unfamiliarity at the time of writing with all but one of the German titles listed in footnote 1, above.

7. David Cesarani, *Final Solution: The Fate of the Jews 1933–1949* (London: Macmillan, 2016), xxxiii; Christian Gerlach, *The Extermination of the European Jews* (Cambridge: Cambridge University Press, 2016), 283–87; Stephan Lehnstaedt, *Der Kern des Holocaust: Belzec, Sobibor, Treblinka und die Aktion Reinhardt* (Munich: C. H. Beck, 2017), 69; and Peter Hayes, *Why? Explaining the Holocaust* (New York: W. W. Norton, 2017), 134–36.

8. Unless otherwise indicated, this paragraph rests on Hayes, *Why?*, 125–27, 131–37.

9. See Deborah Dwork and Robert Jan van Pelt, *Auschwitz: 1270 to the Present* (New York: W. W. Norton & Co., 1996), 168–69, 207–8; Laurence Rees, *Auschwitz: A New History* (New York: Public Affairs, 2005), 20–21, 33–35.

10. Compare the figures in Danuta Czech, et al., *Auschwitz 1940–1945*, vol. V: *Epilogue*, (Oswiecim: Auschwitz-Birkenau State Museum, 2000), 102; and Albert Seaton, *The German Army 1933–45* (New York: St. Martin's Press, 1982), 261.

11. See Mierzejewski, *Asset*, 2:127, and 2:211n70.

12. See Hilberg, "Jewish Souls," chapter 2 in this book.

13. Gottwaldt and Schulle, *Judendeportationen*, 443–67.

14. "Deportation Database and Research Project Online Guide," Yad Vashem, www.yadvashem.org/research/research-projects/deportations/deportation-catalog.

15. Where indicated by an *, the Yad Vashem (YV) Database is the source. For the Netherlands, slightly higher numbers appear in J[acob] Presser, *Ashes in the Wind* (Detroit, MI: Wayne State University Press, 1988), 482–83, and Jules Schelvis, *Sobibor: A History of a Nazi Death Camp* (New York: Berg in association with the United States Holocaust Memorial Museum, 2007), 198–99, but these include small transports and ones destined for sites that were not death camps. For France, the YV database lists seventy-eight transports consecutively numbered by the dispatchers, but trains 14, 34, 41, 43, 54, 56, and 65 are missing from the database. Other sources give numbers ranging from seventy-six to seventy-nine. The French pavilion at the Auschwitz concentration camp lists seventy-three major transports, and I follow its count. For Slovakia, see Schelvis, *Sobibor*, 210–11; Franciszek Piper, *Die Zahl der Opfer von Auschwitz* (Oswiecim: Verlag Staatliches Museum, 1993), 196; and Pätzold and Schwarz, *Nur ein Bahnhof*, 42. For Italy, YV lists only two large transports from the Dodecanese in 1944. I include six others listed by Liliana Picciotto, "Statistical Tables on the Holocaust in Italy with an Insight on the Mechanism of the Deportations," *Yad Vashem Studies* 33 (2005): 322, 334, most of which appear on the YV database but with considerably smaller numbers of people on board. For Hungary, Randolph Braham, *The Politics of Genocide* (Detroit, MI: Wayne State University Press in association with the United States Holocaust Memorial Museum, 2000), 153. For Croatia, Ivo and Slavko Goldstein, *The Holocaust in Croatia* (Pittsburgh, PA: University of Pittsburgh Press in association with the United States Holocaust Memorial Museum, 2016), 365–69, 395–98; and Piper, *Zahl der Opfer*, 196. For Bulgaria (annexed regions), Yitzhak Arad, *Belzec, Sobibor, Treblinka* (Bloomington: Indiana University Press, 1987), 144.

16. Where indicated by an *, the Yad Vashem database is the source. For trains from Warsaw, Yisrael Gutman, *The Jews of Warsaw 1939–1943* (Bloomington: Indiana University Press, 1982), 212. For trains from other sites to Bełżec, Sobibór, and Treblinka, Arad, *Belzec, Sobibor, Treblinka*, 383–95. For trains from other sites to Auschwitz, Piper, *Zahl der Opfer*, 183.

17. See Gottwaldt and Schulle, *Judendeportationen*, 63–64; Engwert and Kill eds., *Sonderzüge*, 61; Mierzejewski, *Most Valuable Asset*, 2:121; Michael Marrus and Robert Paxton, *Vichy France and the Jews* (New York: Basic Books, 1981), 227; and Lucjan Dobroszycki, ed., *The Chronicle of the Lodz Ghetto 1941–1944* (New Haven, CT: Yale University Press, 1984), 125.

18. H.G. Adler, *Theresienstadt 1941–1945* (New York: Cambridge University Press in association with the United States Holocaust Memorial Museum, 2017), 247, 250–51.

19. Franciszek Piper, *Auschwitz 1940–1945*, vol. III: *Mass Murder* (Oswiecim: Auschwitz-Birkenau State Museum, 2000), 40–41; Arad, *Belzec, Sobibor, Treblinka*, 146. The last large transport from Greece, which departed on 2 April 1944, was exceptionally large, however, with eighty wagons; Gerhard Paul and Klaus-Michael Mallmann, eds., *Die Gestapo im Zweiten Weltkrieg* (Darmstadt: Wissenschaftliche Buchgesellschaft, 2000), 425.

20. Arad, *Belzec, Sobibor, Treblinka*, 68, 81; Engwert and Kill, eds., *Sonderzüge*, 58, 61, 70; Mierzejewski, *Most Valuable Asset*, 2:72; Lehnstaedt, *Kern*, 129.

21. Arad, *Belzec, Sobibor, Treblinka*, 136.

22. Passengers: Gall and Pohl (eds.), *Eisenbahn*, 228; Mierzejewski, *Asset*, 146. Cars and Trains: Lichtenstein, *In den Tod*, 22, 26, 126; Pätzold and Schwarz, *Nur ein Bahnhof*, 104–05. Average: Mierzejewski, *Asset*, 145. Produced and Destroyed: Bernhard R. Kroener, et al., *Germany and the Second World War*, vol. 5/2 (Oxford: Clarendon Press, 2003), 498.

23. For the statistics on deportations in Poland that inspire caution about Scheffler's total figure, see Mierzejewski, *Asset*, 2:121; Piper, *Zahl der Opfer*, 183–86; Gottwaldt, *Dorpmüllers Reichsbahn*, 197; Antony Polonsky, *The Jews in Poland and Russia*, vol. 3: *1914 to 2008* (Oxford: Littman Library, 2012), 519; Sara Bender, *The Jews of Bialystok during World War II and the Holocaust* (Lebanon, NH: University Press of New England, 2008), 203, 265.

For the figures regarding military operations, Mierzejewski, *Asset*, 2:78, 2:96–97; Gall and Pohl, *Eisenbahn*, 223, 227; Pätzold and Schwarz, *Nur ein Bahnhof*, 99.

24. Pätzold and Schwarz, *Nur ein Bahnhof*, 105. Their wording in German is: "Keines der zahlreichen Probleme, die es während des Krieges von seinem Beginn bis zu seinem Ende gab, wurde durch die Forderungen des RSHA für die Verwirklichung der 'Endlösung' wesentlich oder auch nur nennenswert verschärft oder hätte durch Verzicht gelöst werden können."

25. Gerlach, *Extermination*, 283.

26. Pätzold and Schwarz, *Nur ein Bahnhof*, 106. That same month, available rolling stock in the east reached "the volume considered adequate . . . for a regular movement of supplies," see Horst Boog, et al., *Germany and the Second World War*, vol. 6 (Oxford: Clarendon Press, 2001), 880–81.

27. Lichtenstein, *In den Tod*, 22, 34, and 95.

28. Ibid., 51.

29. See Engwert and Kill, *Sonderzüge*, 57–60, 70–72, as well as the timetable of 3 August 1942 of a regular train from Warsaw to Treblinka that then returned empty, reproduced on page 61. Also Mierzejewski, *Asset*, 2:117; Lehnstaedt, *Kern*, 128.

30. Lehnstaedt, *Kern*, 68.

31. Lichtenstein, *In den Tod*, 62, 66–67.

32. Robert Kuwalek, *Das Vernichtungslager Belzec* (Berlin: Metropol, 2014), 174.

33. See the descriptions in Bogdan Musial, *Deutsche Zivilverwaltung und Judenverfolgung im Generalgouvernement* (Wiesbaden: Harrassowitz, 2011), 242–44; and Wolfgang Curilla, *Der Judenmord in Polen und die deutsche Ordnungspolizei 1939–1945* (Paderborn: Ferdinand Schöningh, 2011), 442–50; as well as the sequence outlined in the tables provided by Arad, *Belzec, Sobibor, Treblinka*, 393–98.

34. Mierzejewski, *Asset*, 2:121.

35. Ibid., 122; see also Engwert and Kill, *Sonderzüge*, 70, for an example from January 1943.

36. Gottwaldt and Schulle, *Judendeportationen*, 160, 163. See Engwert and Kill, *Sonderzüge*, 73, for the travel plan of train Da52, departing on 22 April 1942, which used wagons that had brought Russians to Germany to take Jews from Dusseldorf to Izbica.

37. Arad, *Belzec, Sobibor, Treblinka*, 52.

38. Gerlach, *Extermination*, 286.

39. Pätzold and Schwarz, *Nur ein Bahnhof*, 92. Note the pleading tone of Himmler's letter to Ganzenmüller of 20 January 1943. [See Document B.6 in this book].

40. See Gottwaldt, *Dorpmüllers Reichsbahn*, 240–41; Mierzejewski, *Asset*, 2:119.

41. See Cesarani, *Final Solution*, 505. Simone Gigliotti, *The Train Journey* (New York: Berghahn, 2009), especially 90–127.

42. Christopher R. Browning, *The Origins of the Final Solution* (Lincoln: University of Nebraska Press, 2004), 42–43; Hans Safrian, *Eichmann's Men* (New York: Cambridge University Press in association with the United States Holocaust Memorial Museum, 2010), 56–57; and Cesarani, *Final Solution*, 259.

43. Michael Alberti, *Die Verfolgung und Vernichtung der Juden im Reichsgau Wartheland 1939–1945* (Wiesbaden: Harrassowitz, 2006), 343; Saul Friedländer, *The Years of Extermination: Nazi Germany and the Jews, 1939–1945* (New York: HarperCollins, 2007), 139.

44. Gerlach, *Extermination*, 284–85; see also Gottwaldt and Schulle, *Judendeportationen*, 88–89; Thomas J. Laub, *After the Fall: German Policy in Occupied France, 1940–1944* (New York: Oxford University Press, 2010), 228–29, 238.

45. Arad, *Belzec, Sobibor, Treblinka*, 50–51; see also Susanne Heim et al. eds., *Die Verfolgung und Ermordung der europäischen Juden durch das nationalsozialistische Deutschland 1933–1945*, vol. 9 (Munich: Oldenbourg, 2014), Document 80, 293–94.

46. Cesarani, *Final Solution*, xxxiii.

47. See Gottwaldt, *Dorpmüllers Reichsbahn*, 197–208; and Alfred Mierzejewski's review of Pasher, *Hitler vs. Wehrmacht* in *Central European History* 49 (2016): 288.

48. See Fedor von Bock, *The War Diary 1939–1945* (Atglen, PA: Schiffer Military History, 1996), 356, entry for 12 November 1941; Browning, *Origins*, 333, 393–94.

49. Mierzejewski, *Asset*, 2:101; Horst Boog et al., *Germany and the Second World War*, vol. 4/2 (Oxford: Clarendon Press, 1998), 1115–17, 1130–31.

50. Cesarani, *Final Solution*, 424.

51. Mierzejewski, *Asset*, 2:102–3; Boog et al., *Germany*, vol. 4/2, 1109–11, 1114–15, 1119, and 1136–37. See also Murray and Millett, *A War to Be Won*, 126–27.

52. Marc Buggeln, *Slave Labor in Nazi Concentration Camps* (New York: Oxford University Press, 2014), 46–49.

53. Gerlach, *Extermination*, 286.

54. Hayes, *Why?*, 135.

55. Horst Boog et al., *Germany and the Second World War*, vol. 7 (Oxford: Clarendon Press, 2006), 598; Richard Overy, *Why the Allies Won* (New York: W. W. Norton, 1996), 167.

56. "Deportation Database," Yad Vashem, www.yadvashem.org/yv/en/about/institute/deportations_catalog_details.asp?country=Thepercent20Netherlands; and Presser, *Ashes*, 482–83.

57. Mierzejewski, *Asset*, 2:104–5.

58. Laub, *After the Fall*, 230; Serge Klarsfeld, ed., *Die Endlösung der Judenfrage in Frankreich: Deutsche Dokumente 1941–1944* (Paris: Beate and Serge Klarsfeld, 1977), 56–57; Gerlach, *Extermination*, 286.

59. See Hayes, *Why?*, 172–74.

Bibliography

Adler, H. G. *Theresienstadt 1941–1945*. New York: Cambridge University Press in association with the United States Holocaust Memorial Museum, 2017.

Alberti, Michael. *Die Verfolgung und Vernichtung der Juden im Reichsgau Wartheland 1939–1945*. Wiesbaden: Harrassowitz, 2006.

Arad, Yitzhak. *Belzec, Sobibor, Treblinka*. Bloomington: Indiana University Press, 1987.

Bender, Sara. *The Jews of Bialystok during World War II and the Holocaust*. Lebanon, NH: University Press of New England, 2008.

Bergen, Doris. *War and Genocide: A Concise History of the Holocaust*, 3rd ed. Lanham, MD: Rowman & Littlefield, 2016.

Bock, Fedor von. *The War Diary 1939–1945*. Atglen, PA: Schiffer Military History, 1996.

Boog, Horst, et al., *Germany and the Second World War*, vol. 4/2: *The Attack on the Soviet Union*. Oxford: Clarendon Press, 1998.

———. *Germany and the Second World War*, vol. 6: *The Global War*. Oxford: Clarendon Press, 2001.

———. *Germany and the Second World War*, vol. 7: *The Strategic Air War in Europe and the War in the West and East Asia, 1943–1944/5*. Oxford: Clarendon Press, 2006.

Braham, Randolph. *The Politics of Genocide*. Detroit, MI: Wayne State University Press in association with the United States Holocaust Memorial Museum, 2000.

Browning, Christopher R. *The Origins of the Final Solution*. Lincoln: University of Nebraska Press, 2004.

Buggeln, Marc. *Slave Labor in Nazi Concentration Camps*. New York: Oxford University Press, 2014.

Cesarani, David. *Final Solution: The Fate of the Jews 1933–1949*. London: Macmillan, 2016.

Curilla, Wolfgang. *Der Judenmord in Polen und die deutsche Ordnungspolizei 1939–1945*. Paderborn: Ferdinand Schöningh, 2011.

Czech, Danuta, et al. *Auschwitz 1940–1945*, vol. 5: *Epilogue*. Oswiecim: Auschwitz-Birkenau State Museum, 2000.

Dobroszycki, Lucjan, ed. *The Chronicle of the Lodz Ghetto 1941–1944*. New Haven, CT: Yale University Press, 1984.

Dwork, Deborah, and Robert Jan van Pelt. *Auschwitz: 1270 to the Present*. New York: W. W. Norton & Co., 1996.

Engwert, Andreas, and Susanne Kill, eds. *Sonderzüge in den Tod*. Cologne: Böhlau, 2009.

Friedländer, Saul. *The Years of Extermination: Nazi Germany and the Jews, 1939–1945*. New York: HarperCollins, 2007.

Gerlach, Christian. *The Extermination of the European Jews*. Cambridge: Cambridge University Press, 2016.

Gigliotti, Simone. *The Train Journey*. New York: Berghahn, 2009.

Goldstein, Ivo, and Slavko Goldstein. *The Holocaust in Croatia*. Pittsburgh, PA: University of Pittsburgh Press in association with the United States Holocaust Memorial Museum, 2016.

Gottwaldt, Alfred. *Dorpmüllers Reichsbahn*. Freiburg: EK, 2009.

———. *Die Reichsbahn und die Juden 1933–1939*. Wiesbaden: Marixverlag, 2011.

———. *Mahnort Güterbahnhof Moabit*. Berlin: Hentrich & Hentrich, 2015.

Gottwaldt, Alfred, and Diana Schulle. *Die "Judendeportationen" aus dem Deutschen Reich 1941–1945*. Wiesbaden: Marixverlag, 2005.

Gutman, Yisrael. *The Jews of Warsaw 1939–1943*. Bloomington: Indiana University Press, 1982.

Hayes, Peter. *Why? Explaining the Holocaust*. New York: W. W. Norton, 2017.

Heim, Susanne, et al. eds. *Die Verfolgung und Ermordung der europäischen Juden durch das nationalsozialistische Deutschland 1933–1945*, vol. 9: *Polen: Generalgouvernement August 1941–1945*. Munich: Oldenbourg, 2014.

Hilberg, Raul. *Sonderzüge nach Auschwitz*. Frankfurt am Main: Ullstein, 1987.

Hildebrand, Klaus. "Die Deutsche Reichsbahn in der nationalsozialistischen Diktatur 1933–1945." In *Die Eisenbahn in Deutschland*, ed. Lothar Gall and Manfred Pohl, 165–243. Munich: Beck, 1999.

Jah, Achim. *Die Deportation der Juden aus Berlin*. Berlin: be-bra wissenschaft verlag, 2013.

Klarsfeld, Serge, ed. *Die Endlösung der Judenfrage in Frankreich: Deutsche Dokumente 1941–1944*. Paris: Beate and Serge Klarsfeld, 1977.

Kroener, Bernhard R., et al. *Germany and the Second World War*, vol. 5: *Organization and Mobilization in the German Sphere of Power*, Part 2: *War Administration, Economy, and Manpower Resources 1942–1944/45*. Oxford: Clarendon Press, 2003.

Kuwalek, Robert. *Das Vernichtungslager Belzec*. Berlin: Metropol, 2014.

Laub, Thomas J. *After the Fall: German Policy in Occupied France, 1940–1944*. New York: Oxford University Press, 2010.

Lehnstaedt, Stephan. *Der Kern des Holocaust: Belzec, Sobibor, Treblinka und die Aktion Reinhardt*. Munich: C. H. Beck, 2017.

Lichtenstein, Heiner. *Mit der Reichsbahn in den Tod*. Cologne: Bund, 1985.

Marrus, Michael, and Robert Paxton. *Vichy France and the Jews*. New York: Basic Books, 1981.

Mierzejewski, Alfred C. *The Most Valuable Asset of the Reich: A History of the German National Railway*, vol. 2: *1933–1945*. Chapel Hill: University of North Carolina Press, 2000.

Murray, Williamson, and Allan R. Millett, *A War to Be Won*. Cambridge, MA: Harvard University Press, 2000.

Musial, Bogdan. *Deutsche Zivilverwaltung und Judenverfolgung im Generalgouvernement.* Wiesbaden: Harrassowitz, 2011.

Overy, Richard. *Why the Allies Won.* New York: W. W. Norton, 1996.

———. *The Bombers and the Bombed: Allied Air War over Europe, 1940–1945.* New York: Viking, 2013.

Pasher, Yaron. *Holocaust versus Wehrmacht: How Hitler's "Final Solution" Undermined the German War Effort.* Lawrence: University Press of Kansas, 2014.

Pätzold, Kurt, and Erika Schwarz. *"Auschwitz war für mich nur ein Bahnhof": Franz Novak— der Transportoffizier Adolf Eichmanns.* Berlin: Metropol, 1994.

Paul, Gerhard, and Klaus-Michael Mallmann, eds. *Die Gestapo im Zweiten Weltkrieg.* Darmstadt: Wissenschaftliche Buchgesellschaft, 2000.

Picciotto, Liliana. "Statistical Tables on the Holocaust in Italy with an Insight on the Mechanism of the Deportations." *Yad Vashem Studies* 33 (2005): 307–46.

Piper, Franciszek. *Die Zahl der Opfer von Auschwitz.* Oswiecim: Verlag Staatliches Museum, 1993.

———. *Auschwitz 1940–1945,* vol. III: *Mass Murder.* Oswiecim: Auschwitz-Birkenau State Museum, 2000.

Polonsky, Antony. *The Jews in Poland and Russia,* vol. 3: *1914 to 2008.* Oxford: Littman Library, 2012.

Presser, J[acob]. *Ashes in the Wind.* Detroit, MI: Wayne State University Press, 1988.

Rees, Laurence. *Auschwitz: A New History.* New York: Public Affairs, 2005.

Safrian, Hans. *Eichmann's Men.* New York: Cambridge University Press in association with the United States Holocaust Memorial Museum, 2010.

Schelvis, Jules. *Sobibor: A History of a Nazi Death Camp.* New York: Berg in association with the United States Holocaust Memorial Museum, 2007.

Schüler, Klaus. "The Eastern Campaign as a Transportation and Supply Problem." In *From Peace to War: Germany, Soviet Russia and the World, 1939–1941,* ed. Bernd Wagner, 205–22. New York: Berghahn, 1997.

Seaton, Albert. *The German Army 1933–45.* New York: St. Martin's Press, 1982.

Torrie, Julia S. *"For Their Own Good": Civilian Evacuations in Germany and France, 1939–1945.* New York: Berghahn, 2010.

Weinberg, Gerhard. *A World at Arms: A Global History of World War II.* New York: Cambridge University Press, 1994.

Photo 1. Albert Ganzenmüller, State Secretary in the Reich Transportation
Ministry and Acting General Director of the Reichsbahn, 1942–45.
Bundesarchiv – Federal Archives. Used with permission.

Photo 2. Julius Dorpmüller, Reich Minister of Transportation, 1937–45. USHMM WS #45272, courtesy of Geoffrey Giles.

Photo 3. Adolf Eichmann, SS Lieutenant Colonel and Leader of
Office IV B 4 (Jews) in the Reich Security Main Office with responsibility for
organizing the Final Solution, in particular all deportation trains departing
from stations outside the General Government, 1941–45.
Sueddeutsche Zeitung Photo. Used with permission.

Photo 4. Franz Novak, SS Captain and Eichmann's assistant with responsibility for transportation and planning, 1941–45. USHMM WS #77643, courtesy of Yad Vashem.

Photo 5. Jews boarding a deportation train from Westerbork transit camp in the Netherlands with the assistance of members of the Jewish Ordedienst. USHMM WS #01340, courtesy of Trudi Gidan.

Photo 6. Jews boarding a deportation train from the Kraków ghetto. USHMM WS #02159, courtesy of Archiwum Dokumentacji Mechanicznej.

Photo 7. Jews boarding a deportation train from the Łódź ghetto to Chełmno. USHMM WS #02625, courtesy of the National Museum of American Jewish History.

Photo 8. Jews boarding a deportation train from an unidentified location in Poland. USHMM WS #05554, courtesy of Leopold Page Photographic Collection.

Photo 9. Jews boarding a deportation train from the Warsaw ghetto with the assistance of members of the Jewish Police. USHMM WS #37288, courtesy of Instytut Pamięci Narodowe.

Photo 10. German Jews assembled for deportation to Riga, Latvia, from Coesfeld, Germany, on 10 December 1941, presumably to go on the train from Düsseldorf described in Documents E.1 and F.1 of this book. USHMM WS #65385A, courtesy of Fred Hertz.

Photo 11. Jews from northeastern Hungary arriving at the ramp at Birkenau, May 1944. USHMM WS #77226, courtesy of Yad Vashem.

INDEX

CPSIA information can be obtained
at www.ICGtesting.com
Printed in the USA
BVHW041128020220
571198BV00016B/952

9 781789 202762